THE NAME GAME

Film moguls of the twenties and thirties manufactured names to fit images and legends: Cary Grant, Lana Turner, Bob Hope, Judy Garland. One Hollywood cowboy was christened John Wayne, or "God has been gracious to wagonmakers." Years later, Wayne is still partial to Western vehicles.

As a theatrical producer, Winthrop Ames learned the value of a good name. He has compiled an extensive catalog of the popular and the picturesque, giving the origin of first names such as Bob, Carol, Ted and Alice as well as Renfred, Outram, Philbert and Hermione. So whether your taste runs to the exotic or the more conventional, there is a name here for you.

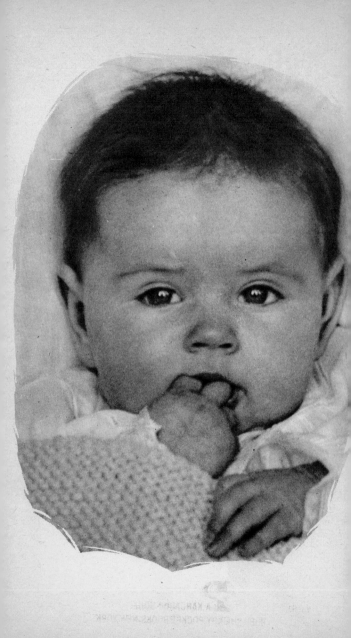

What Shall We Name the Baby?

TWENTY-FIVE HUNDRED BOYS' AND GIRLS' FIRST NAMES
WITH THEIR MEANINGS, DERIVATIONS, NICKNAMES, ETC.

EDITED AND WITH A FOREWORD BY

Winthrop Ames

ASSISTED BY FLORENCE A. DOODY

A KANGAROO BOOK
PUBLISHED BY POCKET BOOKS NEW YORK

WHAT SHALL WE NAME THE BABY?

Fireside edition published 1973

POCKET BOOK edition published September, 1974

This POCKET BOOK edition includes every word contained in the original, higher-priced edition. It is printed from brand-new plates made from completely reset, clear, easy-to-read type.
POCKET BOOK editions are published by
POCKET BOOKS,
a division of Simon & Schuster, Inc.,
A GULF+WESTERN COMPANY
630 Fifth Avenue,
New York, N.Y. 10020.
Trademarks registered in the United States
and other countries.

ISBN: 0-671-80398-0.

Printed in the U.S.A.

Contents

Every child may have an individual ride even if the models differ. . . . were added, clos . . . . and given names were distributed

Foreword

As a theatrical producer I sometimes advised young actors and actresses either to alter their own names or to choose new ones, for a good stage name is a valuable trademark. It should sound well, be easy to remember without seeming tricky or invented, and (because all players, bless them, are certain they will some day become stars) be short enough to display in electric lights. It should also suit the player's personality. Maximilian Hardman hardly seems appropriate for a musical comedy cut-up, nor Nelly Kelley to fit Lady Macbeth. This is why you know John H. Broderibb as "Henry Irving," Sarah Frost as "Julia Marlowe," and the Blythe family as "the Barrymores." I occasionally suggested stage names; and still get a mild thrill when one I coined winks at me from a billboard.

This experience led me to take an interest, first in the sound and aptness of names, then in their derivations and meanings—which is my only excuse for thus venturing to interfere between parents and offspring.

How Names Were Invented

Every child must have an individual title—even a dog needs one so that it may, if so minded, come when you call—and given names were undoubtedly coined almost as soon as men learned to talk. Family names, on the contrary, are only inventions of yesterday in comparison. This seems extraordinary to us, who would find it almost as difficult to get on without our surnames as without our right hands. Indeed, in all except the most intimate relations, surnames have become the more important of the two. Imagine trying to find somebody in New York if the only name he had was John!

But in primitive times when population was sparse, marriage relations loose, and men roved from place to place in quest of crops or game, and had only such inconsiderable possessions to hand down as a bow and arrow or a few clay pots, the family seemed unimportant. The tribe banded together for mutual protection and usually took a title; but a few score names served to distinguish its individual members from one another. The primitive North American Indians were still in this state of civilization; and their way of devising names from some circumstance connected with the child's birth, such as "Great Leaper" or "New Moon," or because of some quality they hoped it might possess, like "Strong Eagle," shows how most appellations were originally invented.

Compare the earliest names in our literature as recorded in the Bible narrative of the creation. If Adam named himself as well as the other animals (I always wonder what names he gave them) he called himself "man of red earth" because he was made of the dust of the earth, and the soil in Palestine is red. Eve, as the mother of all living, was naturally called "life"; and when she saw her first-born, and cried, "I have gotten a man from the Lord!" she called Cain "the gotten." But no one had more than a single name. Down to the time of Christ there were no surnames. He was known only as the Son of Joseph, or, from his birthplace, Jesus of Nazareth, and "of the house of David." Ancestral lines were preserved only in the interminable tables of the Scriptural begats.

FOREWORD

Family Names

It was not until the Romans had become a world power and developed an elaborate civilization that they felt the need of some hereditary title. Then, with characteristic thoroughness, they invented a most complex system; and every patrician Roman traced his descent by taking several names. None of these, however, exactly corresponded to our family name, for the "gens" or clan name was also given to slaves and other dependents. But, though this Roman device suggested the usefulness of surnames, hundreds of years were still to elapse before they came into use. Historians differ as to the exact date, but it was not until after the Norman Conquest, only about nine hundred years ago, that they were at all general in England, or elsewhere in Europe.

Surnames were first taken by the nobles, and indeed were originally spelled "sir names." They were mostly derived from the family's place of abode or stronghold; and a survival of the custom still exists. When a new English peer is created he is given an extra title, usually from his place of residence.

The commoners followed the example of the nobility; but even as late as 1465 surnames were not universal, and Edward V passed a law to compel certain Irish outlaws (who apparently thought it easier to escape identification without a surname) to take them. The wording of this law well illustrates how the new names were devised. It reads: "They shall take unto them a Surname, either of some Towne, or some Colour as Blacke or Brown, or some Art or Science, as Smyth or Carpenter, or some Office, as Cooke or Butler."

Even as late as the beginning of the last century a somewhat similar decree compelled Jews in Germany and Austria to add a German surname to the single names they had previously used. The imagination of the officials entrusted with inventing the new titles accounts

9

for such quaint appellations as "Sweet Child," "Gold Water," "Almond Blossom," "Canary Bird" and the like; and one unfortunate merchant complained that it cost him half his fortune to have the letter "w" put into Schweisshund (bloodhound) and thus avoid being called "dirty dog."

To this day in some remote parts of Ireland surnames are rarely used, and neighbors still call each other by such nicknames as "Michael, son of Big Peg."

The first family names plainly grew out of nicknames (originally called "eke," or added names) based on some personal characteristic of the ancestor. Peter the strong became Peter Strong; black-haired John or blond William became John Black or William White. Others were manufactured by simply adding "son" to the father's name; and Tom's sons became Thompsons, William's sons Wilsons, and so on. The prefixes Fitz and Mac are merely Teutonic and Gaelic for "son." Fitzgerald is Gerald's son; and the Macs and the Mc's, who fill so many columns in our directories, are merely sons of so-and-so. The Irish O' likewise signifies descent. A number of surnames were derived from the trades practiced by the family. Such trade names as Smith, Taylor, Shepherd, Carter, Mason, Miller, etc., interpret themselves. Others may need a word of explanation. Currier was a dresser of skins, Clark a scholar, Webster a weaver, Wainwright a wagon builder, Baxter a baker. Names were also borrowed from birds or animals; and many, like the surnames first taken by the nobles, indicated some place of abode. The original Deans dwelt in a valley, the Shaws in some shady glade, the Greens by the village green, the Atwoods in the forest. The surnames of some of the Pilgrim fathers illustrate such place derivations. John Winthrop's (originally Winthorp) means "from the friendly village"; Governor Endicott's forebears dwelt in an end cottage, Governor Bradford's at a broad ford, and Miles Standish's (whose first name appropriately enough means soldier) were settlers in some stony park.

Indeed scholars have come to believe all English surnames, and most foreign ones, were originally coined either from some bodily characteristic, from the personal name of a sire, from a trade or office, or from a place of residence. Many indicate their origin clearly enough; but others are by no means easy to trace; and glossographers (yes, there are such people) differ about them sometimes with almost spiteful bitterness. My own surname, for instance, has been explained by four learned authorities—all with quite different conclusions.

This discussion of family names may perhaps seem of little assistance in naming a baby; but it will show that surnames, which in recent years are being so much used to vary the endless male parade of Johns and Williams, may be borrowed without fear of infringing any family copyrights. If you choose to call your son Morgan, you may mean (if you feel it necessary to mean anything at all) merely that some ancestor of yours was born by the sea, which is fairly likely. The first Vanderbilts lived near some pile or heap. The Presidency hardly suggests a bed of roses, but the original Roosevelts were Dutch dwellers in a field where roses grew; the Lindberghs came from a mountain slope, and the Fords from some place where one could ford a stream.

Given Names

Given names, on the contrary, date from the very beginnings of language. Every primitive tribe had to invent enough different titles to distinguish its members from one another; and apparently they did so in the same way everywhere, from prehistoric Troy to savage Timbuctoo. They coined them either from some birth-circumstance, some characteristic of the child itself, or some quality they hoped it might possess; they borrowed them from some tribal god; they took them from some strong or swift animal, or some object like a star, a precious stone, a weapon, or a flower. Favorite names were then handed down from generation to generation (their original meaning often forgotten in the process), while others dropped out of use, so that each tribe finally developed its own individual collection. Then, as trade and war brought the nations in contact, they lent and borrowed from one another.

Of the given names used in America today, ninety-nine out of every hundred originated in four mother languages—Hebrew, Greek, Latin (via the Italian, French, etc.), and Teutonic, which last includes such northern tongues as Scandinavian, Old German, Norse, etc.

The Roman rule over the civilized world did much to gather these separately invented names into one general vocabulary. The medieval Church did still more; for after Christianity succeeded Rome as the dominant and uniting power in Europe the Church decreed that her children should be baptized only with names which had been redeemed from paganism by some holy Christian bearer. There was a wide choice, for even the earliest list of saints and martyrs was large, and they came from many nations. Thus a roster of names was established which includes all those in commonest use today. A count of representative pages in the telephone directories of a number of different cities indicates that at least a quarter of all the male citizens in the United States are called either John, William, James, Charles or George; and that one woman in every four answers to Mary, Ann (Anna or Annie), Margaret, Elizabeth or Catherine. These are all saints' names, but they long antedate their saints in origin. William and Charles come from the Teutonic, John and James from the Hebrew, and George from the Greek. Mary, Ann and Elizabeth are Hebrew; Margaret and Catherine Greek,

Name Meanings

It invariably interests anyone to know the significance of his own name, and to trace it back is a fascinating amusement; but, coined in so remote a past, inherited and reinherited so many thousand times, and so transformed by association with famous bearers, it will be obvious that most names have long lost their original meanings. No mother calling her daughter Mary would, with the Virgin Mary intervening, think that she was condemning the child to bitterness; and I suspect the former kind of England, George VI, was not christened with any idea that he was to become a farmer. There is no more likelihood that Maude will prove combative or Winifred peaceful, than that Celia will be blind, or Gladys lame, Paul small of stature, Calvin bald, Philip a lover of horses, or Thomas (if named before birth) turn out to be a twin. The pretty southern Emmylou, which sounds so feminine, literally means "battle ancestress"; and Pollyanna, which most of us associate with a somewhat mulish optimism, signifies "bitter grace."

Indeed, a number of the name meanings given in the following pages may strike the reader as surprising and occasionally even unpleasant. It seems extraordinary that any ancient parent should have chosen to call his son "bear-warrior" (Bernard), or that so lovely a name as Ophelia should mean "snake," but such significations take on a different color when we know their history; and, except in the case of some Hebrew names (for the Israelites appear to have delighted in commemorating their woes), they are almost always intended to be complimentary.

The snake, for instance, seems to have got a bad reputation only in the Garden of Eden. Because snakes periodically cast their skins and apparently emerge as good as new, almost all primitive peoples took them as symbols of immortality, and therefore typical of the wisdom long experience brings. So the serpent rears its head from the royal diadem of Egypt, coils on the shield of Athena the goddess of wisdom, and twines about the caduceus of Apollo the god of healing, and is still today the badge of the physician. Therefore the parents of Ophelia were probably wishing her either eternal youth, wisdom, or beauty—perhaps all three.

The wolf seems to us a predatory animal—but, because of the legendary she-wolf that suckled the deserted twins Romulus and Remus and so enabled them to grow up and found Rome, the wolf became a symbol of national protection to the ancient Romans.

Some Teutonic names bring us pictures of the primitive days in which they were invented. War and hunting were the noblest of occupations, and anything which signified eminence in either was praiseworthy. So "bright or shining spear" might correspond to our "flaming sword" as the badge of an eminent warrior. The stone hurled from a sling was, like the spear, a weapon of conquest and protection, and the name "shining stone" was quite as likely to forecast promise in war as to refer to some much less valuable jewel.

The raven, which so often figures in ancient northern names, was far from being regarded as a bird of ill omen. Twin ravens perched on the shoulders of the great Norse god Odin and served him respectively as mind and memory. The warriors of another Norse god, Thor, had ravens painted on their shields, perhaps to terrify the enemy with the idea that a flock of ravens was coming to pick their bones. So this bird became the badge of a warrior, and the name Bertram ("glorious raven") was probably bestowed in the hope that the lad might become famous in war.

Primitive hunters came to respect the courage of the wild boar, the wolf's cunning, and the bear's strength, and therefore Bernard's parents were probably only wishing him a rugged constitution.

Ancient names, moreover, often take on quite different meanings as they travel down through the ages.

The title Tsar or Kaiser signified imperial power because the Romans, wishing to commemorate Julius Caesar who so widely extended the Roman rule, gave the appellation Caesar to a long line of Roman emperors. But Caesar himself inherited the name because some remote ancestor, who was remarkable for his flowing beard or hair, transmitted his nickname "the long-haired" (which is what Caesar means) to his posterity. Caesar's other name, Julius, was borrowed by still another progenitor from Iulus or Julius, the son of Æneas, in Vergil's *Æneid*. But the name of this youth, just coming into manhood, means "downy-bearded." Thus, if we choose to be literal, we may translate imperious Julius Caesar into "downy-bearded long hair," call July "the downy-bearded month," and Shakespeare's maiden Juliet "little downy-faced girl," and refer to the sword-rattling Kaiser Wilhelm II as "long-haired resolute helmet number two."

In defining names there is always the temptation to make them sound attractive to modern ears—to coo over the cradle as it were. This temptation we have resolutely resisted in the following pages. Besides being honest, a true meaning, when read in the light of its origin, is invariably more interesting.

In christening a child the sentimental association, the sound, and the future usefulness of the name should all be taken into account. If the meaning suits so much the better—if not, it may be disregarded without any serious misgivings.

Fashions in Names

There are, of course, traceable fashions in names, but they are not so extreme or transitory as the fashions in other human habits, because all the most used names are sanctified by tradition and cemented by sentiment. Fashions affect only the fringes as it were. In the United States it is especially difficult to follow any clear trend because the successive waves of immigrants brought their foreign names with them.

The first marked American fashion came from the Puritans. In revolt against the Church of Rome they searched the Old Testament for names not tainted by Popish usage, and unearthed such tongue-twisters as Eliphalet and Bezaleel, along with the more common Aarons, Solomons, and Abijahs. Girls were predirected toward the sterner virtues, such as Prudence, Humility, and Silence; and tradition runs that a third or fourth girl was sometimes called Hopestill because her parents were still hoping for a son. With the wane of Pilgrim authority many of these names gradually passed out of use, though they still survive in New England and in the states colonized from there.

The next trend came with the romantic revival in literature. In the days of our great-grandparents the romantic novels of Richardson, Fanny Burney and Scott and the poetry of Keats, Shelley and Byron were the rage; and thousands of girls were christened Clarissa and Christabel, Gwendolyn and Guinevere. There was less fantasy in the case of boys, but Launcelots and Marmadukes were not unknown. Then the pendulum swung again, and plainer names once more became the vogue.

At the present time there is a marked tendency to supplement the overused standard names with others less usual, though still conservative. Many new and quite charming girl names are being invented, and surnames are more and more being substituted for the overworked Johns and Jameses.

Legalizing Names

Until recent years there was no provision for registering births in many parts of the United States, and our parents often had trouble in getting the equivalent of a birth certificate. Nowadays the attending doctor or midwife is legally obliged to record the date and place of every birth, with the infant's full name if determined. If no first name has yet been chosen the infant is entered as "Girl Smith" or "Boy Jones," and may so remain until some proof of identity, like a birth certificate or marriage license, is required. Then the complete name must be attested and put on record. It is therefore quite possible for especially indulgent parents to allow a child to grow up and then choose his or her own first name. The Catholic Church requires that the children be christened as soon as may be after birth; but even Catholics allow a large assortment of names, such as the English royal family bestow upon their princelings, and so the bearer may still select his own favorite later.

Adults may change both their given and surnames, but only by permission of the Court. Provided there is no intent to evade responsibility or take advantage of another's reputation, and if the reason seems proper, the Courts will usually grant such requests—as in the case of a certain unfortunate gentleman who complained that Adam Herter was no fit title for a dentist.

The Choice of Names

Family tradition is, and probably always will be, the strongest motive in determining what name shall be bestowed upon a child. This is especially true with boys; for marriage may prevent a girl from handing it on intact. By alternating names with every generation, and calling each grandson after his grandfather, the ancient Greeks devised a kind of hereditary chain—a custom still followed in many American families. But the swelling pride of fatherhood seems to produce too large an annual crop of juniors. The sire should be warned of that inevitable day when the son will open his letters; and the son is apt to acquire a nickname that may cling to him through life. I know one important old gentleman who, in his wheelchair, is still called Willie because his father was the William of the family. The senior, too, may some day be slightly downcast to overhear relatives refer to his son as Young Phil, and to himself, though he still thinks himself in his prime, as Old Phil. Any father who expects to become famous should be especially cautioned. I should hate to be known as William Shakespeare, Jr.

A different middle name may avoid this junior difficulty, particularly if the boy is called by it till he is ready to assume his father's title. But with a girl a middle name may be a handicap, for when she marries she might like to keep her family name as the middle one, yet feel some sentimental embarrassment in parting with the other.

There is, of course, only one official Junior in any family—the son who bears the exact name of his father, and during the father's lifetime. Others who inherit the name, such as nephews and grandsons, are distinguished by numbers and called "John Doe 2d" or "John Doe 3d," for example.

With girls it is easy to transmit a favorite name without always repeating it exactly, for the number of variants of some of the standard female appellations is surprising. There are, for instance, no less than a score of different ways of calling a girl either Mary or Elizabeth or Anna or Rose. And almost every male name has at least one, and often several, pleasant feminine equivalents.

Some circumstance of birth may occasionally suggest an unusual or appropriate name. Noel and Natalie signify Christmastide; April, May and June recall pleasant months; Dominic means Sabbath-born; Neoma is born under a new moon; Nerissa smacks of the sea, etc. In former days classical-minded parents sometimes gave their children Greek or Latin number names; and there is the tale of an English parson who, having called his first-born Primus, the second Secundus, and so on up to Decima, the tenth, christened the next girl Ultima, or "the last," in despair—though with what success is not recorded.

FOREWORD

It is always difficult to imagine that an infant, fighting an imaginary punching-bag and blowing bubbles in its bassinet, will ever grow up into, say, an admiral with epaulettes, or the dean of a woman's college with queenly manners and a transformation; but such possibilities should be faced. A six-foot Amazon may not be grateful that she was named Ninette; nor an overportly gentleman care to be reminded of the fact whenever his friends call him Percy.

As even the dignity of the presidential office does not prevent Abraham from being shortened to Abe, Theodore to Teddy and Calvin to Cal, it is well to reflect what abbreviation a name is likely to have. For there are good and bad nicknames—some ludicrous, some so ingratiating as to be social assets. It is said that President Wilson felt he might have been more generally popular if his first name could have been abbreviated to anything but Woodie or Row. Parents may sometimes forestall an undesirable nickname by inventing one of their own and applying it to the youngster in advance. And such nursery appellations as Brother or Sistie should be firmly eradicated before they become indelible.

Name Sounds and Rhythms

A name that does not clearly indicate its pronunciation by its spelling may prove a life-long nuisance. I know a certain Gerald who spends precious hours expostulating that his name does not begin with a "j"; Americans usually omit the final "e" in Irene, though it is sounded in England; and Miss Ina Claire tells me that half her acquaintances call her "Eenah" and the other half "Eynah." She answers docilely to either.

To begin both a first name and a surname with the same letter, as in Henry Hale or Emily Ellis, often results in a combination which, though the alliteration sounds attractive at first hearing, may prove too artificial and calculated to wear well. On the other hand, the same sounds in the *unaccented* syllables of both names makes for harmony. Much of the music of Ann Hathaway, for example, comes from the echo of the initial A in the unaccented syllables of Hathaway.

If a surname happens to be undistinguished it is wise to keep the given name simple. Gloriana Potts or Orlando Stubs seem—well, a little anti-climactic.

The euphonious sound of the whole name depends more upon the proper balance between the syllables of the first and the last names than on any other single factor. A one-syllable first name joined to a single-syllable last name (Mae West, Ed Wynn), in spite of its occasional style and snappiness, is rarely musical. To my ear, the best combination with a one-syllable last name is a three-syllable first name. For example, I like the sound of Elinor Brown better than Nell Brown, or Ellen Brown, or Eleanora Brown. With a two-syllable last name I prefer a three-syllable first name—Elinor Browning sounds better than Nell Browning or Ellen Browning or Eleanora Browning. With a three-syllable last name I like a single-syllable first name, although a two-syllable first name is also rhythmically pleasant, and both Nell Brownington and Ellen Brownington are good. But Elinor Brownington and Eleanora Brownington seem over-weighted. Using any of these rhythmic patterns—three-syllable first names with both one and two-syllable last names, and one or two-syllable first names with a three-syllable surname—you will have to be somewhat ingenious to invent a really ill-sounding combination. The same patterns, of course, hold good for boy names. An initial, if used constantly as part of the whole, has the effect of adding an extra syllable to the first name. John D. Rockefeller counts as a two and four-syllable combination.

How to Use This Book

Intended to suggest names for present day use, those listed in the following pages were compiled mainly from recent directories and "Social Registers" of various representative cities. Names of historic interest only, which have outlived their popularity, are omitted. It was thought few modern parents would care to call a boy Pompey or a girl Ethelburga, important as those appellations once were. On the other hand, many novel and attractive names, either recently coined or revived from old sources, have been included. And in the male section will be found a large number of surnames already in use as given names, and which are becoming increasingly popular.

The Name Meanings

It would be pure hypocrisy to pretend that all the interpretations of names given in this—or in any other —book can be warranted accurate. Although most names have fairly clear pedigrees, there are others, invented so long before writing, and so altered by mouth-to-mouth transmission and by adoption into various languages, that they can be translated only by more or less educated guess-work. In such cases we have tried to follow those authorities whose guesses seemed best founded. And if some of the meanings given are set

21

down with undue assurance the fault is mine, not that of my collaborator, Miss Florence A. Doody, who has done the lion's share of the research—if lions do research. Indeed, I have sometimes had to tie her hands to prevent her from tucking a cautious "probable" or "possible" into some definition that seemed to me sufficiently reliable.

Language Sources

For the language source of a name we have tried to cast back to the tongue—sometimes only a root-word—from which it sprang. Lillian, for instance, though its present form comes from the Latin, originated in Greek and is therefore so attributed.

Under "Teutonic" are grouped the ancient interrelated languages of Northern Europe, such as Norse, Scandinavian, Old German, Dutch, etc., occasionally even reaching into the Anglo-Saxon. "Old English" covers the dialects between Anglo-Saxon and modern usage. "Celtic" stands for early Irish, Welsh and Scottish.

Residence and Occupation Names

Those labeled "Residence Names" are derived from the place of residence or abode of some ancestor. Most of these were originally nicknames which later became surnames. An "Occupation Name" signifies one given to a forebear because of the trade, business or art he practiced.

Diminutives

The only abbreviation used is DIM. for diminutives. Under this head are listed not only nicknames and other actually shortened forms, but sometimes also those which carry the meaning or suggestion of littleness. Marietta, for instance, is a true diminutive of Mary although it has more letters, because the "etta" means "little." The feminine suffixes "ette," "etta," "ella," "elle," and usually "ine" and "ina," as well as the Slavonic "ka," all carry this diminutive significance.

Authorities

To list the authorities we have consulted would require too many pages. They range from personal letters to a treatise on cuneiform inscriptions. Those interested in name-study will find a very complete and up-to-date bibliography in Flora Haines Loughead's "Dictionary of Given Names" (A. H. Clark Co., Glendale, Cal.). The best authority on surnames is Henry Harrison's "Surnames of the United Kingdom" (London, 1912-1918). And no investigator should fail to pay tribute to Charlotte M. Yonge's "History of Christian Names" (Macmillan, N. Y., 1878), the pioneer work in English.

Winthrop Ames
September, 1934.

Girls' Names

Girls' Names

A

Abigail .... "Source of joy" (*Hebrew*). Literally, "father of joy"; but "father" in the Hebrew is equivalent to "source." DIM. Abby, Abbie, Gail.

Accalia .... In Latin tradition Accalia was the foster-mother of Romulus and Remus, founders of Rome.

Ada .... "Happy or prosperous" (*Teutonic*).

Adabel, Adabelle .... Ada and Belle combined, so meaning "happy and fair."

Adah .... "Ornament" or "beauty" (*Hebrew*).

Adalia .... "Noble" (*Teutonic*).

Adamina .... The feminine of Adam, which in Hebrew means "man of red earth."

Adela .... See Adelaide, below.

Adelaide .... "Noble, and of good cheer" (*Teutonic*). DIM. Adela, Adèle, Addie, Addy, Alice, Elsie, Elsa.

Adèle .... A French form of Adelaide, above.

Adeline, Adaline, Adelina .... Forms of Adelaide, above.

Adine, Adina .... Feminine forms of Adin, which means "delicate" (*Hebrew*).

Adria .... Feminine of Adrian. A famous Latin name of unknown meaning. It survives in the Adriatic Sea.

Adrienne, Adriane, Adriana .... French, German and Italian forms, respectively, of Adria.

Agatha .... "The good" (*Greek*).

27

WHAT SHALL WE NAME THE BABY?

Agna ... A diminutive of Agnes, below.

Agnella ... An Italian form of Agnes, below.

Agnes ... "Pure, gentle, meek" (*Greek*). In Latin the word means "lamb"; and on St. Agnes' feast day lambs are still blessed by the Pope. There is a superstition that maidens may discover their future lover by performing certain rites on St. Agnes' Eve. DIM. Agna, Neysa, Inez.

Agneta ... A form, originally Swedish, of Agnes, above.

Aileen ... "Light" (*Greek*). An Irish form of Helen.

Ailsa ... Probably, like Elsa, a variant of Adelaide, meaning "noble, and of good cheer" (*Teutonic*).

Aimée ... "Beloved" (*French*).

Airlia ... "Ethereal" (*Greek*).

Alanna, Alane ... "Comely or fair" (*Celtic*). Feminine forms of Alan.

Alarice ... Feminine of Alaric, which means "ruler of all" (*Teutonic*).

Alberta, Albertine, Albertina ... "Noble and brilliant" (*Teutonic*). Feminine forms of Albert.

Alcina ... Feminine of Alcinous, a Greek legendary king. In Ariosto's "Orlando Furioso" Alcina is a fairy who changed her lovers into trees and animals.

Alda ... "Rich" (*Teutonic*).

Aldea ... A variant of Alda, above.

Aldercy ... A name of modern coinage, perhaps based on the Old English proper name, Alder, meaning "chief or prince."

28

Aldis, Aldys .... Originally an Old English "residence" surname, meaning "from the old house."

Aldora .... "Winged gift" (*Greek*).

Aleris .. An ancient Greek name, from a now vanished city on the island of Corsica.

Alethea .... "Truth, sincerity" (*Greek*).

Aletta, Aleta .... "The winged" or "bird-like" (*Latin*).

Alexa .... A diminutive of Alexandra, below.

Alexandra .... "Helper of Mankind" (*Greek*). Feminine of Alexander. DIM. Alexa, Alexina, Alexine.

Alexandrina .... A variant of Alexandra.

Alexine, Alexina .... Diminutives of Alexandra.

Alfreda .... "Supernaturally wise" (*Teutonic*). The feminine of Alfred.

Alice .... "Noble, and of good cheer" (*Teutonic*). Originally a shortened form of Adelaide, but used as an independent name. DIM. Alla, Allie.

Alicia, Alisa .... Forms of Adelaide, through Alice, above.

Alida, Aleda .... From Alida, a city in Asia Minor where splendid garments were manufactured. So the name might fancifully be translated "the richly clad."

Alina .... "Comely or fair" (*Celtic*).

Alison .... "Of sacred fame" (*Teutonic*).

Allegra .... "Sprightly and cheerful" (*Old French-Latin*). In his poem "The Children's Hour" Longfellow nicknamed one of his daughters "laughing Allegra."

Allis, Alyce, Alys .... Varied spellings of Alice, above.

Alma .... "The fostering or nourishing" (*Latin*); or "learned" (*Arabic*).

Almeta .... "Pressing toward the goal," or "ambitious" (*Latin*).

Almira .... "The exalted, or a princess" (*Arabic*).

Alodie .... "Wealthy or prosperous" (*Anglo-Saxon*).

Aloys, Aloyse .... Diminutive forms of Aloysia, below.

Aloysia .... "Famous in war" (*Teutonic*). Feminine of Aloysius.

Alphonsine, Alfonsine .... "Eager for battle" (*Teutonic*). Feminine forms of Alphonso.

Althea .... "Wholesome or healing" (*Greek*). A "flower" name. The althea, or "Rose of Sharon," is a plant supposed to have medicinal power.

Altheda .... A varied spelling of Althea, above.

Alva .... "White or fair" (*Spanish-Latin*).

Alvina .... "Beloved by all" (*Teutonic*). Feminine of Alvin.

Alvita .... "Vivacious, animated" (*Latin*).

Alysia .... "Captivating, or binding" (*Greek*).

Alyssa .... Probably a form of Alicia, or Alice, meaning "noble, and of good cheer" (*Teutonic*). Possibly from the flower "alyssum."

Amabel, Amabelle .... "Loveable" (*Latin*). The second form carries the added meaning of "beautiful."

Amadis .... "Love of God" (*Latin*).

Amalea, Amalia, Amélie .... The first two are Italian, the last a French form of Amelia, below.

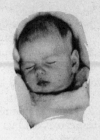

Amalthea .... A name which may be interpreted as
"god-nourishing." Amalthea was the legendary
goat who suckled Zeus, father of the Greek gods.

Amanda .... "Worthy of love, loveable" (*Latin*). DIM.
Manda, Mandy.

Amara Either "unfading" (*Greek*); or from Amara,
a paradise in Abyssinian legend.

Amarantha .... A "flower" name. In Greek the amaranth
means "the unfading, or immortal."

Amaris .... "Whom God hath promised" (*Hebrew*).
From the Biblical name Amariah.

Amaryllis .... "Fresh, or sparkling" (*Greek*). A favorite
name with poets for a fresh country girl. Also a
"flower" name.

Amber .... A "jewel" name. Amber was esteemed by
the ancients not only as a semi-precious jewel but
for its supposed curative properties. The word is
Arabic.

Ambrosine .... "Immortal" (*Greek*). The feminine of
Ambrose.

Amelia .... A name of puzzling significance. It comes
from Æmilius, an ancient Roman family. Their
name may be most safely translated as "industrious, or laboring"; though they themselves interpreted it as "persuasive or flattering," from some
golden-tongued ancestor.

Amethyst .... A name from the precious stone, anciently
worn as a charm against intoxication (*Greek*). It
is the February birth stone.

WHAT SHALL WE NAME THE BABY?

Amity .... "The friendly" (*Latin*).

Amorette .... "Little love, or sweetheart" (*Latin*). A name probably invented by Spenser for a loving wife in his "Faerie Queene" (1590).

Amorita .... "Beloved" (*Latin*).

Amy .... "Beloved" (*Latin*). Sometimes also used as a short form of Amelia, though this gives it a different meaning.

Anastasia .... "One who shall rise again" (*Greek*). The feminine of Anastasius.

Ancelin .... "Handmaid" (*Old French-Latin*).

Andrea, Andreana .... Feminine forms, the latter Italian, of Andrew.

Andromeda .... The name of a maiden in Greek mythology. To punish her mother, who had boasted of the girl's beauty, she was chained to a rock to be devoured by a sea-monster, but was rescued by Perseus.

Angela .... "The angelic" or "the heavenly messenger" (*Greek*).

Angelica .... An Italian form of Angela, above.

Angelina, Angeline .... Forms of Angela, above.

Angelita .... A diminutive, or "pet," form of Angela, above.

Anita .... "Grace" (*Hebrew*). A form, originally Spanish, of Ann.

Anitra .... A form of Anita, above.

Ann, Anne .... "Grace, mercy, or prayer" (*Hebrew*). Originally Hannah. As commemorating St. Anne, mother of the Virgin Mary, these names have become favorites in all Christian countries. DIMINUTIVES AND VARIANTS: Annie, Annetta, Annette, Anita, Annice, Nan, Nana, Nanny, Nancy, Nanine, Nanette, Ninette, Nina, Ninon, Nanon.

Anna .... A form, originally Latin, of Ann, above.

Annabel, Annabelle .... In modern usage "fair Anna"— a combination of Anna and Belle. But these names may also signify "joy" if traced back to a Gaelic origin.

Annette, Annetta .... Diminutive forms of Ann, above.

Annice .... An old English variant of Ann, above.

Annora, Anora .... A combination of Ann and Nora, so meaning "grace and honor."

Anona .... Probably from Annona, the Latin goddess of the annual yield of fruits or produce.

Anselma ... "Divine protectress" (*Teutonic*). Feminine of Anselm.

Anstice, Anstace .... "One who shall rise again" (*Greek*).

Anthia, Anthea "Flower-like" (*Greek*).

Antoinette .. "Beyond praise" (*Latin*). A French feminine diminutive of Antony. DIM. Toinette.

Antonia, Antonina .... "Beyond praise" (*Latin*). The first is an Italian, the second an English, feminine form of Antony.

33

WHAT SHALL WE NAME THE BABY?

April .... From the month. The Latin word "aprilis" means "open"—that is, when the earth opens for the growth of spring.

Ara .... Either "eagle maid" (*Teutonic*), or "an altar" (*Latin*).

Arabella .... Either "eagle heroine" (*Teutonic*), or "fair altar" (*Latin*).

Araminta .... Probably "an Aramean," from the ancient race which inhabited what is now Syria. The meaning of their name is doubtful. It may signify "lofty" (*Hebrew*).

Ardath .... A name given in the Apocryphal Bible to "a flowering field."

Ardelis .... "Zealous or industrious" (*Latin*).

Ardelle, Ardella .... "Zealous or ardent" (*Latin*).

Ardine, Ardene .... Forms of Ardis, below.

Ardis .... "Fervent or eager" (*Latin*).

Ardith .... "Rich gift" (*Teutonic*), from an Anglo-Saxon form of Edith.

Ardra .... "The ardent or eager" if from the Latin. If from the Celtic "high, or noble."

Areta, Aretta, Arette .... Of doubtful meaning. Perhaps forms of Aretina, below.

Aretina .... "The virtuous" (*Greek*).

Ariadne .... In Greek mythology the daughter of the sun-god, honored as a goddess and as the personification of spring. The name probably means "most holy" (*Greek*).

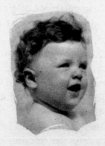

Ariana .... "Silvery" (*Welsh*).

Ariella .... Formerly the feminine of Ariel, a Biblical name meaning "lion of God" (*Hebrew*); but since Shakespeare in "The Tempest" called his fairy spirit of the air by this title it has come to signify "ethereal."

Arilda .... "Hearth, or home, maid" (*Teutonic*).

Arlana .... "A pledge" (*Celtic*). A feminine form of Arlen.

Arlene, Arlena, Arleen .... "A pledge" (*Celtic*). Feminine forms of Arlen.

Arleta, Arlette .... Elaborated forms of Arlene, above.

Arline, Arlina .... "A pledge" (*Celtic*). The name Arline was made popular by Balfe's opera "The Bohemian Girl" of which she was the heroine.

Armilda .... "Armed battle-maid" (*Teutonic*).

Armilla .... "A bracelet" (*Latin*).

Arnoldine .... "Mighty as the eagle" (*Teutonic*). Feminine of Arnold.

Arva, Arvia .... Perhaps "fertile," from the Latin word meaning "a ploughed field."

Aspasia ... "The welcome" (*Greek*). Aspasia, the mistress of Pericles of ancient Athens, was famous for her intelligence and charm.

Astra, Astrea .... "Starlike" (*Greek*). Astræa was the goddess of justice in Greek mythology, who, after a stay on earth, returned to heaven and became the constellation Virgo.

Astrid, Astred .... Either "impulsive in love" (*Teutonic*), or forms of Astra, above.

Atalanta .... In Greek legend, the name of a beautiful and swift-footed huntress.

Atalaya .... "A watch-tower" (*Spanish-Arabic*).

Atalie .... Probably a shortened form of Athalia, below; though it may be a form of Hatili, a Swiss diminutive of Catherine, and so mean "pure."

Athalia .... "The Lord is mighty" (*Hebrew*). Athalia was a famous queen of Judah in Bible history.

Athena, Athene .... Implying "wisdom," from the Greek Athena, goddess of wisdom.

Auberta .... "Noble and brilliant" (*Teutonic*). The feminine of Aubert, a French form of Albert.

Audrey .... "Nobly strong" (*Teutonic*). St. Audrey's name survives in our word "tawdry," because cheap finery was sold at fairs held on her feast day.

Audris .... "Fortunate or wealthy" (*Teutonic*).

Augusta .... "The exalted, sacred, or sublime" (*Latin*). The feminine of Augustus. The title Augusta was conferred by Roman emperors on their wives and daughters.

Augustine, Augustina .... Forms of Augusta, above.

Aurea .... "The aureate, or golden" (*Latin*).

Aurelia .... "Golden" (*Latin*).

Austine, Austina .... "The exalted" (*Latin*). Feminine forms of Austin.

Avis .... Either "a bird" (*Latin*), or an Old English form of Hedwig meaning "refuge in battle" (*Teutonic*).

Azalea, Azelia .... Either "spared by Jehovah" (*Hebrew*), or a "flower" name from the blossom of the evergreen shrub.

B

Babette .... Used in English as a "pet" diminutive for Barbara, but in French as a diminutive of Elizabeth.

Baptista, Battista .... "The baptizer" (*Greek*). A name commemorating St. John the Baptist. Battista is the Italian form.

Barbara .... "The stranger." From the word applied by the ancient Greeks to anyone who did not speak their language—not necessarily a barbarian. DIM. Bab, Babs, Babette.

Bathilda, Bathilde .... "Commanding battle-maid" (*Teutonic*). The second is a French form.

Bathsheba .... "Daughter of an oath" or "a pledge" (*Hebrew*). A Biblical name.

Beata .... "Blessed" (*Latin*).

Beatrice, Beatrix .... "She who blesses, or makes happy" (*Latin*). DIM. Bee, Trix, Trixy.

Becky .... "The ensnarer" (*Hebrew*). A short form of Rebecca, which see.

Bee .... A "pet" name for Beatrice, although nowadays occasionally used as an individual name.

Belda .... A contraction of "belle dame," or "fair lady" (*French*).

Belinda .... A name made fashionable in England by the heroine of Pope's poem "Rape of the Lock." It literally means "serpent-like" (*Italian*); but the ancient serpent symbolized both wisdom and immortality. See Foreword.

Bella .... "Beautiful" (*Latin*). Also a diminutive of Isabella, which see.

Belle, Bell .... "Beautiful" (*Latin*). Also contractions of Isabella, which see.

Benedetta .... "The blessed." An Italian feminine form of Benedict.

Benedicta .... "The blessed" (*Latin*). A feminine of Benedict.

Benetta .... "The blessed" (*Latin*). A short form of Benedetta.

Benita .... "The blessed" (*Latin*). A Spanish feminine form of Benedict.

Berdine .... "Bright maiden" (*Teutonic*).

Bernadette .... A French diminutive of Bernard. St. Bernadette is the saint who saw the vision of the Virgin at Lourdes, France.

Bernardine, Bernardina .... Feminine forms of Bernard. The masculine name means "brave, or bear-strong, warrior" (*Teutonic*).

Berneta, Bernetta, Bernette .... Feminine diminutives of Bernard.

Bernice, Berenice .... "Bringer of victory" (*Greek*).

Bertha, Berta .... "Bright or glorious" (*Teutonic*). Berta is also sometimes used as the feminine for Albert, etc. See Bertina.

Bertilde .... "Commanding battle-maid" (*Teutonic*). Another form of Bathilda.

Bertina .... "Bright, or shining" (*Teutonic*). Also a feminine diminutive for Albert, Bertram, Herbert, Hubert, etc.

Beryl .... A "jewel" name. The beryl was a precious stone worn in the breastplate of the Hebrew high priest. It was probably the topaz, although the emerald and aquamarine are also varieties of beryl.

Bess .... "Consecrated to God" (*Hebrew*). A contraction of Elizabeth. Queen Elizabeth I of England was popularly called "Good Queen Bess."

Beth .... "House, or home" (*Hebrew*). Also used as a short form of Elizabeth.

Bethesda .... "House of mercy," or "place of flowing water" (*Hebrew*). Bethesda was the name of a pool in Jerusalem the waters of which became healing when stirred by an angel.

Betsy, Betty, Bett, Bette .... Some of the many short forms of Elizabeth. An old English riddle-rhyme goes:

"Elizabeth, Betsy, Beth, Betty and Bess
All went out together to take a bird's nest;
They came on a nest that had six eggs in,
And each took one out, yet they left five in!"

Bettina, Bettine .... Forms of Elizabeth, meaning "consecrated to God" (*Hebrew*).

Beulah, Beula — "She who is to be married" (*Hebrew*). A Biblical name for the Land of Israel (Isaiah lxii:4).

Bianca — "The white, or fair" (*Teutonic-Latin*). A Spanish form of Blanche.

Billie — A feminine nickname from William, sometimes used as an independent name.

Bird — A modern name, suggesting bird-like qualities.

Blanche, Blanch — "White, or fair" (*Teutonic-Latin*). Blanche was originally the French form, Blanch the English.

Blanda, Blandina — "Affable, seductive, or flattering" (*Latin*).

Blenda — "Dazzling, or glorious" (*Teutonic*).

Blossom — A modern name, carrying its own suggestion.

Blythe — "Glad or joyous" (*Anglo-Saxon*).

Bonnibel, Bonnibelle — "Good and beautiful" (*Latin*).

Bonny, Bonnie — "Sweet and fair" (*French-Latin*).

Brenda — The feminine of Brand, a Teutonic masculine name which means either "sword" or "firebrand."

Brenna — "Raven maid" (*Celtic*). The raven was a bird highly esteemed among the ancients. See Foreword.

Briana — "The strong" (*Celtic*). The feminine of Brian.

Bridget — "The strong" (*Celtic*). St. Bridget is a favorite patron saint of Ireland.

Brita, Brietta — Forms of Bridget, above.

Brunhilda, Brunhilde .... A heroine of Norse mythology who lay asleep in a circle of flame till roused by her suitor. The name literally means "battle-maid with the breastplate" (*Teutonic*).

C

Calandra .... "The lark" (*Greek*).

Calida, Callida .... "The ardent" (*Latin*).

Callista, Calista .... "The most beautiful" (*Greek*).

Calvina .... Feminine of Calvin.

Camilla, Camille .... In Latin mythology Camilla was an attendant, famous for swiftness of foot, on the goddess Diana. Later any attendant at a sacred rite was so called. Camille is a French form.

Candice, Candace .... "Glowing" (*Latin*).

Candida "The white, or pure" (*Latin*).

Cara "Friend" (*Celtic*).

Carilla A feminine form of Charles, based upon the old Spanish form Carillo.

Carin, Caryn, Carina .... Carina "the keel" (*Latin*) is one of the five stars in the constellation Orion, all of which are named from the parts of a ship.

Carisa .... "Artful" (*Latin*).

Carita .... "The charitable" (*Latin*).

Carla A feminine diminutive of Charles.

Carlen, Carleen, Carlin .... Shortened and "pet" forms of Caroline, which is the feminine for Charles.

WHAT SHALL WE NAME THE BABY?

Carlina .... A shortened form of Carolina, feminine for Charles.

Carlita, Carletta .... Diminutive feminine forms of Carl, or Charles.

Carlotta .... An Italian form of Charlotte. This name was first introduced to France, and thence to England, by the wife of Louis XI. DIM. Lotta, Lotty.

Carmel, Carmela .... From the Biblical Mt. Carmel in Palestine, famous for the deeds of the prophets Elijah and Elisha, and the site of the original Carmelite monastery. In Hebrew "carmel" means "woodland, or park."

Carmen .... A favorite Spanish name of three possible meanings; either "rosy" or "a song" if from the Latin, or "vine-dresser" if from the Hebrew.

Carmita .... A diminutive, or "pet," form of Carmen, above.

Carol .... "Song of joy" (*Old French*). Also used as a diminutive of Caroline.

Carola .... A diminutive of Carolina, and a feminine of Charles.

Caroline, Carolyn, Carolina .... Feminine forms of Charles. The states of Carolina were named for King Charles II of England. DIM. Carrie, Lina.

Carrie .... A diminutive of Caroline, above.

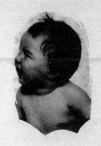

Cary, Carey .... Either varied spellings of Carrie, and so diminutives of Caroline; or, if derived from the Celtic, meaning "the dark"—of hair or complexion.

Casilda . A Spanish name of undetermined meaning. A Cuban seaport is so called.

Cassandra In Greek mythology, a prophetess whose true forebodings were never believed.

Cassie .... "Pure" (*Greek*). A diminutive of Catherine. Also, though rarely, used as a diminutive of Cassandra.

Catalina .... "Pure" (*Greek*). A Spanish form of Catherine.

Caterina .... "Pure" (*Greek*). An Italian form of Catherine.

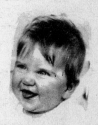

WHAT SHALL WE NAME THE BABY?

Catherine, Catharine, Catharina .... "Pure" (*Greek*). A name, with many forms and diminutives, popular in all European languages. It was originally spelled with a K, but as the Anglo-Saxons did not have that letter, C became the early English substitute. The first three of the following variants may be also spelled with a C. DIMINUTIVES AND VARIANTS: Katrine, Katrina, Kathleen, Kate, Kathie, Katie, Kitty, Kit, Cassie, Trine, Trina, Trinette.

Cathleen, Cathlin .... "Pure" (*Greek*). Usually Irish endearing forms of Catherine. But they may also be traced to the Celtic name of a star, meaning "beam of the wave."

Cécile, Cecily, Cicily, Cecil .... Forms, the first French, of Cecilia, below.

Cecilia .... Literally "blind" (*Latin*); but the name was a favorite among the ancient Romans, and now especially commemorates St. Cecilia, the virgin martyr who sang while being tortured, and became the patron saint of music. DIM. Sisely, Cissy, Cis.

Celena .... In Greek mythology Celæno was one of the seven daughters of Atlas, who, as stars, became the Pleiades.

Celeste, Celesta .... Forms, the first French, of Celestine, below.

Celestine .... "Heavenly" (*Latin*).

Celia .... A short form of Cecilia, above.

Celina .... From Selene, the goddess of the moon in Greek mythology.

Cerelia .... An Italian form of Ceres, the Roman goddess of the harvest; so perhaps signifying "fruitfulness."

Chanda .... One of the names assumed by Devi, "the great goddess" (*Sanskrit*), in Hindu mythology.

Chandra .... "Eminent or illustrious." The Sanskrit name for the moon, which, as it outshines the stars, took this meaning.

Charis .... One of the Three Graces of Greek mythology, especially associated with the grace of charity.

Charity .... "Benevolent, charitable, loving" (*Latin*). A favorite Puritan "virtue" name.

Charlene, Charline .... Diminutives of Charlotte, and feminine forms of Charles.

Charlotte .... The feminine of Charles. DIM. Carry, Lotta, Lotty.

Charmian, Charmion .... An attendant on Cleopatra, mentioned by Plutarch and used as a character by Shakespeare in "Antony and Cleopatra."

Cherry .... A short form of Charity, above.

Cheryl .... The feminine of an old German form of Charles.

Chloe .... "Blooming or verdant" (*Greek*). The summer name of Demeter, the Greek goddess of agriculture. (Compare Melanie.) Chloe was a favorite name with poets for a fresh rustic maiden.

Chloris .... The goddess of flowers in Greek mythology, corresponding to Roman Flora. Pursued by Apollo she turned white, whence her name "the pale" (*Greek*).

WHAT SHALL WE NAME THE BABY?

Chriselda .... A form of Griselda, which see.

Christa .... "The Christian, or anointed" (*Greek*). A short form of Christina.

Christabel, Christabelle .... "Fair Christian"; that is, Christian with the feminine suffix meaning "fair."

Christel, Christal .... Scotch feminine forms, usually for Christian, but sometimes for Christopher.

Christiane, Christiana .... "The Christian, or anointed" (*Greek*). Feminine forms of Christian. The name Christiana was popularized by Bunyan in "Pilgrim's Progress."

Christina, Christine .... "The Christian, or anointed" (*Greek*). Feminine forms of Christian. DIM. Christa, Chrissie, Tina.

Clara .... "Bright or illustrious" (*Latin*). Made famous by St. Clare of Assisi, who founded the first order of nuns. Also used as a feminine of Clarence.

Clare, Claire .... "Bright or illustrious" (*Latin*). Forms, the second French, of Clara.

Clarette .... A "pet" or diminutive form of Clara, above.

Claribel, Clarabelle .... "Bright and fair" (*Latin*). Clara, with an added ending meaning "beautiful."

Clarice .... A French form of Clarissa, below.

Clarinda .... "Bright and fair" (*Latin*). An English form of Clara, invented in the eighteenth century.

Clarine .... A diminutive, or "pet," form of Clara, above.

Clarissa .... "Making famous" (*Latin*). A name fashionable in the eighteenth century because of Richardson's novel "Clarissa Harlowe."

Clarita, Clareta .... Elaborated forms of Clara, above.

Claudette .... A diminutive form of Claudia, below. The "ette" means "little."

Claudia .... "Lame" (*Latin*). The feminine form of Claude.

Claudine, Claudina .... The first French, the second the Italian form of Claudia, above.

Clematis .... "The vine, or clinging" (*Greek*). A "flower" name.

Clementine, Clementina .... "The merciful" (*Latin*). Feminine forms, the first French, of Clement.

Cleo .... "The famous" (*Greek*). Also a diminutive of Cleopatra, below.

Cleopatra The name has come to suggest seductive charm from Egypt's famous queen. Literally it means "her father's fame" (*Greek*).

Clorinda A name probably coined by the Italian poet Tasso for his heroine in "Jerusalem Delivered" (1581)—a maiden who preferred military prowess to love.

Clotilde, Clotilda .... "Famous in battle" (*Teutonic*). The first Clotilda was the Christian wife of Clovis, king of the Franks, who persuaded him to adopt her faith, and so influenced the history of Western Europe. Clotilde is a French form.

Clover .... A name, originally Anglo-Saxon, from the clover blossom.

Clyte .... A nymph in Greek mythology beloved by Apollo the sun-god. She was changed into the heliotrope, a flower which was supposed to turn always toward the sun.

Colette, Collette .... "A necklace" (*French-Latin*).

Colleen .... "Girl" (*Irish*).

Columbine .... "The dove" (*Latin*). A "flower" name from the columbine, the blossom of which is supposed to resemble a group of doves. The name first appears in an old Italian comedy where Columbine is the coquettish sweetheart of Harlequin.

Comfort .... A favorite Puritan "virtue" name.

Connie .... Short for Constance, below.

Constance .... "The constant, or firm of purpose" (*Latin*). A favorite name with several English poets, generally for a devoted woman.

 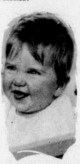

Constantia, Constancia .... The first a Latin, the second a Portuguese, form of Constance.

Consuela, Consuelo .... "Consolation" (*Latin*). The name Consuelo was made fashionable by George Sand's novel of that title (1842).

Cora .... "Maiden" (*Greek*). Short for Corinna.

Coral .... From the coral of the sea (*Greek*). Coral was anciently worn as a charm because it was supposed to lose color at the approach of evil spirits or sickness.

Coralie, Coraline .... Elaborated forms of Coral, above.

Cordelia .... An old Celtic name, perhaps to be translated "jewel of the sea." Made famous by Shakespeare in "King Lear," in which Cordelia is the dutiful daughter.

Corella .... Either an elaborated form of Cora, or a combination of Cora and Ella.

Coretta, Corette .... "Little maid." Diminutive forms of Corinna, below.

Corinna, Corinne .... "Maiden" (*Greek*). Corinna was a noted Greek lyric poetess; Corinne was the heroine of a fashionable novel by Madame de Staël (1807).

Cornelia Feminine of Cornelius, which see. Cornelia was an historic Roman matron of wifely virtues, who, when reproached for her plain attire, exhibited her children, exclaiming, "These are my jewels!"

Crystal .... "Crystal" or "brilliantly pure." Derived from the Greek word meaning "frost."

Cynara .... A classic Greek name, probably from an island in the Aegean Sea now called Zinara.

Cynthia ... One of the titles of the Greek moon-goddess Artemis, and so poetic for "the moon."

Cyrene, Cyrena .... The name of a water-nymph in Greek mythology.

Cytherea, Cytheria .... In Greek mythology one of the titles of Aphrodite, or Venus, from the island of Cythera, where she is supposed to have been born of the sea-foam.

D

Dacia .... An ancient Latin name derived from the Roman province of Dacia. Any further significance is unknown.

Daffodil .... A "flower" name. A Greek fable relates that daffodils were originally white, but turned yellow when touched by Pluto as he was carrying off Persephone, a maiden who was gathering them. In the underworld they were changed into asphodels.

WHAT SHALL WE NAME THE BABY?

Dagmar .... "Joy of the Danes" (*Danish*). A name commemorating a much beloved Danish queen.

Dagna .... "Fair as the day" (*Teutonic*).

Daisy, Daisie .... A "flower" name from the daisy—in Anglo-Saxon "day's eye." It became a nickname for Margaret because its French form, Marguerite, is the French name for the daisy.

Damalis .... "The tamer or conqueror" (*Greek*).

Damara .... A shorter form of Damaris, below.

Damaris .... "The gentle or mild" (*Greek*), from the qualities of the heifer, which the Greek word literally means.

Danette .... A feminine diminutive of Daniel, which means "God is my judge" (*Hebrew*).

Danica .... "The morning star" (*Slavonic*).

Daniela, Danila .... "God is my judge" (*Hebrew*). Feminine forms of Daniel.

Danita .... A feminine diminutive of Daniel, meaning "God is my judge" (*Hebrew*).

Daphne .... "The laurel tree" (*Greek*). In Greek mythology Daphne was a nymph transformed into a laurel tree when fleeing from the god Apollo.

Dara .... "The heart of wisdom" (*Hebrew*).

Daralis, Daralice .... "Beloved, or dear" (*Old English*).

Daria, Darya .... "A queen, or queenly" (*Persian*). Feminine forms of Darius, which means "the king."

Darice .... "The queen, or queenly" (*Persian*). A feminine form of Darius.

Darlene, Darline .... "The tenderly beloved" (*Anglo-Saxon*).

Daryl .... "Beloved or dear" (*Old English*).

Davina .... "The beloved one" (*Hebrew*). A feminine of David.

Dawn .... "The break of day" or "awakening" (*Anglo-Saxon*).

Deborah .... "The bee" (*Hebrew*). In ancient Egypt the bee was a symbol of regal power. With the Greeks it symbolized prophecy; and the Biblical prophetess Deborah was accordingly so called.

Decima .... "The tenth" (*Latin*). A name sometimes given to a tenth child, in days when families were so afflicted.

Deirdre . In ancient Irish folklore Deirdre was a maid of great beauty, but fated to cause misfortune. Her name in Gaelic means "sorrow."

Delcine, Dulcine ... Modern variants of the Spanish Dulcinia, which means "sweet or delightful" (*Latin*).

Delia .... A name given to the Greek moon-goddess Artemis, from the island of Delos, her supposed birthplace. Also used as a short form of Cordelia.

Delicia ... "Charming, or delightful" (*Latin*).

Delilah, Dalila .... The name in Hebrew means "pining with desire"; but, because of the Biblical Delilah who betrayed Samson, it has come to signify "temptress."

Della .... A form of Delia, above; although also used as an independent name.

Delora .... "From the seashore" (*Latin*).

Deloris .... A form of Dolores, which see.

51

WHAT SHALL WE NAME THE BABY?

Delphine, Delphina .... A name probably derived from the world-famous Delphic Oracle of Apollo in Greece. It may also mean "dolphin," the symbol of a calm sea in Greek mythology.

Demetria .... A form of Demeter. Demeter was the Greek goddess of fertility and harvests.

Denise, Denice, Denys .... French feminine forms of Dennis, which is derived from Dionysos, the Greek god of wine.

Desirée .... "The desired, or longed-for" (*French-Latin*).

Desma .... "A pledge, or bond" (*Greek*).

Desmona .... "Ill-starred" (*Greek*). A contraction of Desdemona, which Shakespeare chose for the name of his ill-fated heroine in "Othello."

Devona .... "The defender" (*Anglo-Saxon*). The English county of Devonshire was so called because its inhabitants bravely defended themselves from a Danish invasion.

Diana, Diane .... In Roman mythology Diana was the virgin goddess of the moon.

Dianthe, Diantha .... A "flower" name from the pink, or dianthus, which in Greek means "divine flower."

Diella, Dielle .... "Worshipper of God" (*Latin*).

Dinah, Dina .... "The judged, vindicated, or avenged" (*Hebrew*).

Dione, Diona .... In Greek mythology Dione was the daughter of heaven and earth, and the mother of Aphrodite.

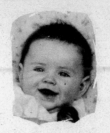

Dionis .... A Spanish form of Dione, above.

Dixie .... "Girl from the South." A slave dealer named
Dixie once owned a plantation in New York City.
Here the slaves were so well treated that, when
sold, they looked back on Dixie's Land as a sort
of paradise, and made songs about it. From these
songs the name came to be applied to the Southern states.

Docilla, Docila .... "The docile, or teachable" (*Latin*).

Dolly, Dollie, Doll .... Affectionate diminutives, or nicknames, for Dorothea which means "divine gift"
(*Greek*).

Dolores .... A favorite Spanish name, commemorating
the Virgin Mary as the "Mater Dolorosa" or "Our
Lady of Sorrows."

Dolorita .... A diminutive, affectionate form of Dolores,
above.

Domela .... "Mistress of the home" (*Latin*).

Dominica .... "The Lord's" (*Latin*). A name often given
to girls born on Sunday, or the Lord's Day. Feminine of Dominic.

Donalda .... The feminine of Donald, which see.

Donata .... "A gift" (*Latin*).

Donella .... Either "little mistress" (*Latin*), or "dark-
haired elfin girl" (*Celtic*).

Donia .... If from the Latin this name means "a gift";
if from the Celtic "of dark, or brown, complexion."

Donica .... "A gift" (*Latin*).

Donna .... "Lady, or mistress." An Italian feminine
form of the Latin word for "lord."

Dora .... "A gift" (*Greek*). An individual name, but also used as a diminutive of Dorothea, Theodora, Eudora, etc.

Doralia, Dorelia .... "A gift" (*Greek*). Elaborated forms of Dora.

Doralis, Doralice .... "A gift" (*Greek*). Elaborated forms of Dora.

Dorcas .... "The gazelle" (*Greek*). The word literally means "with large dark eyes." The name has come to signify "charitable" because of the Dorcas in the New Testament who made garments for the poor.

Dorcea, Dorcia .... Modern forms of Dorcas, above.

Dorette .... "Little gift." A diminutive, or "pet," form of Dora.

Doria, Dorea .... Either forms of Doris, below; or feminine forms of Dorian, which see.

Dorice .... Either a form of Doris, below; or a feminine form of Dorian, which see.

Doris .... "Of the sea." In Greek mythology Doris was a sea goddess, and mother of the sea nymphs.

Dorita .... "Divine gift" (*Greek*). A diminutive of Dorothea.

Dorlisa .... "Divine gift" (*Greek*). A German form of Dorothea.

Dorothea, Dorothy .... "Divine gift" (*Greek*). Feminine forms of Theodore.

Drusilla, Drucilla .... "Dewy eyes" (*Greek*).

Dulcia, Dulcea .... "Sweet, or delightful" (*Latin*).

Dulcie, Dulcy :.. Forms of Dulcia, above.

E

Easter .... A name sometimes given to a child born at Easter-tide. The word Easter comes from the name of the Anglo-Saxon goddess of spring, which in turn was taken from Eos, the Greek goddess of dawn.

Eberta .... "Formidably brilliant" (*Teutonic*). The feminine of Egbert.

Echo .... In Greek mythology, Echo was a nymph who pined away from unrequited love till only her voice remained.

Eda .... "Happy, prosperous, rich" (*Anglo-Saxon*).

Edana .... "Ardent or fiery" (*Celtic*). The feminine of Edan.

Edeline .... "Noble, and of good cheer" (*Teutonic*). A varied spelling of Adeline.

Eden .... "Delightful or pleasant" (*Hebrew*). The Garden of Eden signified "pleasantness."

Edina .... "Prospering and happy" (*Anglo-Saxon*). Also a poetic name for the City of Edinburgh.

Edith .... "Rich gift" (*Teutonic*); or "prospering and happy" (*Anglo-Saxon*). Both sources give much the same meaning.

Editha, Edita .... Forms of Edith, above.

Edla .... A shortened form of Edlyn, below.

Edlyn .... "Noblewoman, or princess" (*Anglo-Saxon*).

Edmée .... "Prosperous protector" (*Anglo-Saxon*). A French feminine form of Edmond.

Edmonda, Edmunda .... "Prosperous protector" (*Anglo-Saxon*). Feminines of Edmund.

Edna .... "Pleasure or delight" (*Hebrew*). The name of the Garden of Eden is derived from the same word.

Edolie .... Perhaps a varied modern spelling of Adela, which means "noble, and of good cheer" (*Teutonic*).

Edra, Edrea .... Either "mighty" (*Hebrew*); or if from the Teutonic "prosperous."

Edris .... A feminine form of Edric, which means "prosperous ruler" (*Anglo-Saxon*).

Edwina .... "Valuable friend" (*Anglo-Saxon*). The feminine of Edwin.

Effie .... "Of fair fame" (*Greek*). A short form of Euphemia.

Eglantine .... The sweet-briar, or wild rose (*Old French*). A "flower" name.

Eileen .... "Light" (*Greek*). An Irish form of Helen or Eleanor.

Elaine .... "Light" (*Greek*). A form of Helen or Eleanor. In the King Arthur legends Elaine was the "lily maid" who pined and died for love of Launcelot.

Elata .... "The exalted or triumphant" (*Latin*).

Elberta .... "Nobly brilliant" (*Teutonic*). The feminine for Elbert.

Eldora .... Probably a contraction of Eldorado, "the golden or gilded" (*Spanish*). Eldorado was first applied by the Spanish conquerors to a South American chief who powdered himself with gold dust as a religious rite. The word came to signify any golden or desirable land.

Eldoris .... Either a form of Doris, meaning "of the sea" (*Greek*), or of Eldora, above.

Eldrida .... "Sage counselor" (*Anglo-Saxon*). The feminine of Eldred or Eldrid.

Eleanor, Eleanora "Light" (*Greek*). Derived from Helen, which see. DIM. Ellen, Eileen, Nell, Nelly, Lena. Nora, though sometimes used as a diminutive, comes properly from Honoria.

Electra .... "The bright or shining" (*Greek*). A "star" name. In Greek mythology Electra was one of the seven sister stars of the Pleiades. Another Electra was a favorite heroine in Greek tragedies.

Elena .... An Italian form of Helen, meaning "light" (*Greek*).

Eleonora, Eleonore .... "Light" (*Greek*). Forms, originally Italian and German respectively, of Helen.

Elfrida, Elfreda .... "Supernaturally wise" (*Teutonic*). Feminine forms of Alfred, which see.

Elga Probably a varied spelling of Olga, meaning "holy" (*Teutonic*); but if derived from the Anglo-Saxon it means "elfin spear."

Elinor, Elenor .... "Light" (*Greek*). Varied spellings of Eleanor.

Elisabet .... A Greek form of Elizabeth, below.

Élise A French diminutive form of Elizabeth, below.

Elissa, Elisia .... Varied and contracted spellings of Elizabeth, below.

Elita .... "The chosen or selected" (*Old French-Latin*).

Eliza .... "Consecrated to God" (*Hebrew*). A short form of Elizabeth, but also used as an individual name.

Elizabeth, Elisabeth .... Literally "God of the oath" (*Hebrew*)—that is, "one consecrated by oath to God." Commemorates St. Elizabeth, mother of John the Baptist, and kin to the Virgin Mary. A name highly popular in all European languages, as may be seen from its many forms. DIMINUTIVES AND VARIANTS: Elisabetta, Elsbeth, Elspeth, Elsabet, Eliza, Elise, Elsie, Lizzie, Lise, Lisa, Libby, Betsey, Betty, Bessie, Bess, Beth, Bettina.

Ella .... "Elfin" (*Anglo-Saxon*). In olden days elves were esteemed as supernatural beings who sometimes influenced and advised mortals.

Elladine .... A name of modern coinage, perhaps based upon Ella, above.

Ellamay, Ellamae .... A modern combination of Ella and May.

Ellen .... "Light" (*Greek*). A form, originally Scotch but long adopted into English, of Helen.

Ellette .... "Little elf." A "pet" form of Ella.

Ellice .... The feminine of Elias or Ellis, which mean "Jehovah is God" (*Hebrew*).

Elma .... "Amiable" (*Greek*). The masculine form of this name was borne by St. Elmo who was supposed to warn sailors of impending storms.

Elmina .... "Of awe-inspiring fame" (*Teutonic*). Feminine of Elmer. It may also be an Anglo-Saxon "tree" name from the elm.

Elna .... "Light" (*Greek*). A contraction of Eleanor.

Elnora .... "Light" (*Greek*). A shortened form of Eleanora.

Elodie .... A "flower" name, from the white blossom of
the water-thyme.

Eloine .... "Worthy to be chosen" (*Latin*). A name
commemorating St. Eloi, or Eloy, a famous ancient goldsmith saint and the patron of workers in
the precious metals.

Eloïse .... "Famous in battle" (*Teutonic*). Like Heloïse,
a French form of Louise.

Elora .... "Light" (*Greek*). A shortened form, through
Elnora, of Eleanora.

Elsie, Elsa .... Contractions, the latter German, either
of Adelaide or of Elizabeth.

Elspeth .... "Consecrated to God" (*Hebrew*). A Scotch
abbreviation of Elizabeth.

Elva, Elvia .... "The elfin" (*Anglo-Saxon*).

Elvina .... "Befriended by the elves" (*Anglo-Saxon*).
The feminine of Elvin or Elwin.

Elvira, Elvera .... "The white or fair" (*Latin*).

Emelda .... A name of uncertain derivation.

Emeline, Emelina, Emelin .... "Industrious" (*Teutonic*).
Forms of Emily.

Emera .... Either "industrious" (*Teutonic*), or "deserving" (*Latin*).

Emily .... "Industrious" (*Teutonic-Latin*). A shorter,
and Teutonic, form of Amelia, which see.

Emlyn .... "Industrious" (*Teutonic*). A form of Emily.

Emma .... "Ancestress, or grandmother" (*Teutonic*).
Though an independent name, it is sometimes used
as a form of Emily, which would give it a different significance.

Emmylou .... A modern combination. If literally translated it signifies "an ancestress famous in battle."

Enid .... "The soul or spirit" (*Celtic-Latin*). The story
of the fair and virtuous Enid of the King Arthur
legends is told by Tennyson in his "Idylls of the
King."

Enrica, Enrika .... "Ruler of the home" (*Teutonic*).
Feminines of Henry through a Spanish form.

Erica, Erika .... "Ever powerful, or regal" (*Teutonic*).
Feminines of Eric.

Erina .... "Girl from Ireland." Erin is the ancient Celtic,
and still the poetic, name for Ireland.

Erlina, Erline .... Either meaning "the elfin" (*Anglo-
Saxon*), or varied spellings of Arlina and Arline,
which mean "a pledge" (*Celtic*).

Ermina .... "Noble" (*Latin*). Also sometimes used as a
short form of Hermione, which see.

Erna .... A contraction of Ernesta, below.

Ernesta .... "Intent in purpose" (*Teutonic*). Feminine
for Ernest.

Ernestine .... "Intent in purpose" (*Teutonic*). Feminine
for Ernest.

Esma, Esme .... Perhaps contractions of Esmeralda,
below; or feminine forms of Esmond, "gracious
protector" (*Anglo-Saxon*).

Esmeralda .... "The emerald" (*Spanish-Greek*). A
"jewel" name.

Essie .... A nickname for Esther, below.

Estelle .... "A star" (*Latin*). The French form of Stella.

Esther .... "A star." A Biblical name which can be traced through the Hebrew, Latin, and Greek to the Persian, in which it probably signified the planet Venus. DIM. Essie, Hetty.

Estra .. Probably "goddess of spring," or Easter (*Anglo-Saxon*); possibly a form of Esther.

Estrella .... An elaborated Spanish form of Esther, above.

Ethel .... "Noble" (*Teutonic*).

Ethelda .... "Noble in counsel" (*Teutonic*).

Ethelind .... "Nobly wise" (*Teutonic*)—literally "noble serpent," but the serpent anciently signified both wisdom and immortality.

Etta .. A diminutive, usually of Henrietta which means "mistress of the home" (*Teutonic*); but it may also be a diminutive for several other names. By itself it merely means "little."

Eudocia, Eudosia, Eudoxia .... "The esteemed, or honored" (*Greek*).

Eudora .... "Good, or delightful, gift" (*Greek*).

Eugenia, Eugénie .... "The well-born" (*Greek*). Feminine forms, the latter French, of Eugene.

Eulalia, Eulalie .... "Fair of speech" (*Greek*). Eulalie is a French form.

Eunice .... "Happily victorious" (*Greek*). In the Bible Eunice is referred to as "of assured faith" (II Timothy i:5).

Euphemia, Euphemie .... "Of fair fame" (*Greek*). DIM. Effie, Phemie.

Eurydice .... In Greek mythology the wife of Orpheus. Returning with him from the underworld she was snatched away because he broke his promise not to look back.

Eva .... "Life" (*Hebrew*). Originally the Greek and Latin form of Eve.

Evadne .... A favorite name in classic Greek poetry and mythology. One Evadne was a water-nymph; another a wife who sacrificed herself on her husband's funeral pyre.

Evangeline .... "Bearer of glad tidings" (*Greek*). The popularity of this name was revived by Longfellow's poem "Evangeline" (1849).

Evania .... "Tranquil, or untroubled" (*Greek*).

Evanthe .... "A flower" (*Greek*).

Eve .... "Life" (*Hebrew*). "And Adam called his wife's name Eve, because she was the mother of all living." (Genesis iii:20.)

Eveleen .... An Irish form of Evelina, below.

Evelina, Eveline, Evelyn .... These names are now generally considered as elaborations of Eve ("life"); but there are older Celtic forms which mean "pleasant or agreeable." DIM. Lena, Lina.

F

Fabrienne .... The feminine of Fabron, which see.

Faith .... "The believing or faithful" (*Latin*). A "virtue" name.

Fanchon .... "Free" (*Teutonic*). A French feminine diminutive of Francis.

Fania, Fanya .... Slavonic equivalents of Fanny, below.

Fanny, Fannie .... "Free" (*Teutonic*). Diminutive forms of Frances, though also used as independent names.

Farica .... "Peaceful ruler" (*Teutonic*). An English spelling of Feriga, the Italian feminine diminutive for Frederick.

Fausta .... Short for Faustina, below.

Faustina, Faustine ... "The fortunate" (*Latin*).

Fawnia, Faunia ... "A fawn, or young deer" (*Old French-Latin*).

Fay, Fae, Faye .... Either "fairy" (*Old French*), or a diminutive of Faith, above.

Fayette .... A form of Fay with a diminutive ending meaning "little."

Fayre .... "The beautiful or comely." An Old English spelling of "fair."

Fedora .... "Divine gift" (*Greek*). A Russian form of Theodora.

Felda .... "A field" (*Teutonic*).

Felicia, Félice, Félise ... "The fortunate or happy" (*Latin*). Feminine forms of Felix.

Felita .... A form of Felicia, above.

Fenella .... "The white-shouldered" (*Celtic*).

Fern .... A "plant" name. The Greek word for fern means "a feather."

Fernanda, Fernande .... "Adventurous in life" (*Teutonic*). Feminine forms of Ferdinand.

Fidelia .... "The faithful" (*Latin*).

Fidelity .... "Faithfulness" (*Latin*). A Puritan "virtue" name.

Fifi .... A contraction of Fifine, below.

Fifine .... A French diminutive of Josephine, which means "He shall add" (*Hebrew*).

Fiona .... "The white or fair" (*Celtic*).

Flavia .... "Blonde, or yellow-haired" (*Latin*).

Fleda .... Another spelling of Fleta, below.

Fleta .... "The fleet, or swift" (*Teutonic*).

Fleur .... "A flower" (*French-Latin*).

Fleurette .... "Little flower" (*French*).

Flora .... "A flower" (*Latin*). Flora was the Roman goddess of spring and flowers.

Florella .... "Flowering or blooming" (*Latin*).

Florence .... "Flowering or blooming" (*Latin*). In Irish use, however, this name may be derived from a Celtic word meaning "fair child."

Floria .... "Flowering" (*Latin*). A form of Flora.

Florida .... "The flowering or blooming" (*Latin*). The Southern state of Florida was so named because it was discovered on Easter Day, which in Spanish is called "Pascua florida" or "flowering Easter."

Floris .... "A flower" (*Latin*). Another form of Flora.

Fonda .... "The profound, or well-based" (*Spanish-Latin*).

Fortuna, Fortune .... "The fortunate" (*Latin*). Fortuna was the Roman goddess of good luck.

Frances .... "Free" (*Teutonic*). Feminine of Francis, which see for fuller definition. DIM. Fanny, Fran.

Francesca, Francisca .... "Free" (*Teutonic*). Italian and Spanish feminine forms of Francis, which see.

Francine .... "Free" (*Teutonic*). A feminine diminutive of Francis, which see.

Freda, Frida .... "Peaceful" (*Teutonic*). An individual name, but sometimes also used as a feminine contraction of Frederick.

Fredella .... A modern name, probably Fred and Ella combined. If so it may be translated "peaceful elf."

Frederica, Fredrika .... "Peaceful ruler" (*Teutonic*). Feminine forms of Frederick.

Fritzi, Fritzie .... Feminine forms of Fritz, which means "peaceful ruler" (*Teutonic*).

Frodine, Frodina .... "Wise, or learned, friend" (*Teutonic*).

Fronia .... From the Latin word meaning "forehead," so figuratively signifying "wise" or "intelligent."

Fulvia .... "The blonde, or yellow-haired" (*Latin*).

G

Gabrielle, Gabriella .... "God is my strength" (*Hebrew*). Feminine forms of Gabriel.

Galatea .... In Greek mythology an ivory statue of a maiden brought to life by Aphrodite at the prayer of the sculptor Pygmalion. The name may come from the Greek and mean "milk-white."

Gale .... "Gay or lively" (*Old English*).

Garda .... "The protected or guarded" (*Teutonic*). Our word "garden" has the same original meaning.

Gavra .... Short for Gavrila, below.

Gavrila, Gavrilla .... "God is my strength" (*Hebrew*).
Feminine forms, originally Slavonic, of Gabriel.

Gay .... "Lighthearted or merry" (*French-Teutonic*).

Geneva .... Either a short form of Geneviève, below;
or "the juniper" (*Old French*). The city of Geneva
was named from the juniper tree.

Geneviève .... Probably "white wave" (*Celtic*). In the
fifth century the city of Paris was saved from its
assailants by the prayers of a shepherd girl of this
name, and she became its patron saint.

Genevra .... An Italian form of Geneviève, above.

Georgette .... A French feminine diminutive of George,
which means "husbandman" (*Greek*).

Georgia .... Feminine of George, which means "husbandman" (*Greek*).

Georgiana .... Feminine of George, which means "husbandman" (*Greek*).

Georgina .... A shorter form of Georgiana, above.

Geralda, Giralda .... "Mighty with the spear" (*Teutonic*). Feminine forms of Gerald.

Geraldine .... "Mighty with the spear" (*Teutonic*).
Feminine of Gerald.

Gerda .... "The guarded or protected" (*Teutonic*).
Our word "garden"—literally an enclosed or protected place—comes from the same root.

Germaine .... "A German." The origin of the German
national name is obscure. It has been variously
interpreted as "armed" or "spear-people" (*Teutonic*); as "neighbors," or again as "the shouters"
(*Celtic*).

66

Gertrude .... "Spear maiden" (*Teutonic*). In Norse mythology the name of one of the Valkyrs, maidens who bore the souls of slain warriors to Valhalla. DIM. Gertie, Trude, Truda, Trudy.

Gilberte, Gilberta .... "Illustrious pledge, or hostage" (*Teutonic*). Feminine forms of Gilbert, although this is one of the few cases in which the female form antedates the male.

Gilda .... "Servant of God" (*Celtic*).

Glad .... "Merry, or glad" (*Old English*). Also used as a short form of Gladys.

Gladys .... "Lame" (*Latin*). A Welsh feminine form of Claudius, or Claude.

Glen, Glenn .... Short forms of Glenna, below.

Glenna .... "From the glen or valley" (*Gaelic*). A "residence" name.

Glennis .... A form of Glenna, above.

Gloria .... "The glorious" (*Latin*).

Gloriana, Gloriane, Glorianna .... A compound of Gloria and Anna, thus meaning "of glorious grace." In his "Faerie Queene" (1590) Edmund Spenser eulogized Queen Elizabeth I as Gloriana, queen of fairy-land, and made the name popular in England.

Grace .... "The graceful" (*Latin*). The Three Graces of classical mythology typified respectively beauty, joy, and grace. See Gratiana.

Gracia .... An English variant of the Italian Grazia, or Grace.

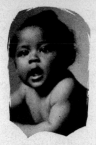

Grania .... "Love" (*Celtic*). A popular heroine in Gaelic folklore.

Grata, Gratia ... Shorter forms of Gratiana, below.

Gratiana .... A Latin form of Grace. The Latin root from which the word comes may signify not only "grace," but "divine favor," "esteem," "kindness" or "thankfulness."

Gredel .... "A pearl" (*Greek*). A German diminutive, originally Grethel, of Margaret.

Greta .... "A pearl" (*Greek*). Originally a Slavonic diminutive of Margareta.

Gretchen .... "Little pearl." A German diminutive of Margaret.

Griselda .... Literally either "stone heroine" or "gray-haired heroine" (*Teutonic*); but from the story of Griselda, as related by Boccaccio, Petrarch, Chaucer and others, the name has become synonymous with patience and wifely obedience.

Griseldis ... Another form of "the patient Griselda," above.

Grizel, Grissel .... Forms, the first Scotch, of Griselda, above.

Guinevere, Guenevere .... "White or fair lady" (*Celtic*). The wife of King Arthur in the Round Table legends, for love of whom Sir Launcelot failed in his search for the Holy Grail.

Gustava .... Feminine of Gustavus, which see.

Gustel .... "The exalted" (*Latin*). A short German form of Augusta.

Gwen, Gwenn .... "The white or fair" (*Celtic*). An independent name, but also used as short for Gwendolen and Guinevere.

Gwendolen, Gwendolin, Gwendolyn .... "White-browed" (*Celtic*). But the name may also be derived from that of an ancient British goddess corresponding to Diana, and so signify "lady of the bow."

Gweneth, Gwenith .... Probably "white or fair," but possibly also "blessed" (*Celtic*).

Gwynne, Gwyn .... "White or fair" (*Celtic*).

Gypsy, Gipsy .... "A Gypsy." The Gypsy race, though originally Hindu, were supposed to come from Egypt, whence their name. It has come to signify "a Bohemian" or "rover."

H

Hagar .... "Flight" (*Hebrew*). The Biblical Hagar was so called because she fled from her mistress Sarai into the wilderness.

Haldis .... "Stone spirit" (*Teutonic*). The stone occurs frequently in old Teutonic names. It may stand for a weapon, or signify firmness. See Foreword.

Halette .... Feminine, with a diminutive suffix meaning "little," of Hal, which see.

Hally, Hallie .... Diminutive feminine forms of Henry or Harold, which see.

Halona .... "Of happy fortune" (*American Indian*).

Hannah .... "Grace, mercy, or prayer" (*Hebrew*). For variants and diminutives see Ann.

Happy .... A modern "pet" name of obvious meaning.

Harelda, Haralda .... Feminine forms of Harold, which means "mighty in battle" (*Teutonic*).

Harriet, Harriette, Harrietta .... "Mistress of the home" (*Teutonic*). Feminine forms of Henry, though also used as independent names.

Hatty, Hattie .... "Mistress of the home" (*Teutonic*). Diminutives for Harriet and Henrietta.

Hazel .... "Commander" (*Teutonic*). A wand of the hazel tree was the symbol of authority with ancient shepherd chiefs.

Heather .... A "flower" name from the heather, or flowering heath.

Hebe .... The personification of youth. In Greek mythology Hebe was cupbearer to the gods, and goddess of youth and spring.

Hedda .... A short German form of Hedwig, below.

Hedwig .... "Refuge in battle" (*Teutonic*).

Helen .... "Light" (*Greek*). A favorite name, made famous by the legendary Helen of Troy, celebrated for her beauty and charm, whose abduction by Paris caused the Trojan War. Her name comes originally from the Greek sun-god, Helios, or "light." For diminutives see Eleanor.

Helena, Hélène .... The first is the Latin, the second a French, form of Helen, above.

Helenka .... "Light" (*Greek*). A Polish form of Helen. The "ka" is diminutive.

Helga .... "Holy" (*Teutonic*).

Heloïse .... A French form of Louise, meaning "famous in battle" (*Teutonic*). The name was made popular in France by the romantic love-story of Abelard and Heloïse.

Helsa .... "Consecrated by oath to God" (*Hebrew*). A short Danish form of Elizabeth.

Henrietta .... "Mistress of the home" (*Teutonic*). Feminine of Henry. DIM. Hatty, Hattie, Etta.

Henrika .... A Swedish feminine form of Henry, which means "ruler of the home" (*Teutonic*). .

Hephzibah, Hepsiba .... "My delight is in her" (*Hebrew*). A Biblical name.

Hepzibeth .... A form of Hephzibah, above.

Hera .... Hera was the queen of the gods in Greek mythology, and patroness of womanhood and maternity.

Hermandine .... Probably derived from Hermes; see Hermione, below. Also used as a feminine for Herman.

Hermia .... A contraction of Hermione, below.

Hermione   In Greek mythology Hermione was the daughter of Helen of Troy. Her name is the feminine for Hermes, messenger of the gods and patron of travelers. His name probably means "of the earth" (*Greek*).

Hertha .... "Mother earth." In Teutonic mythology Hertha was the earth goddess, and symbolized fertility.

Hesper .... "The evening star" (*Greek*).

Hester .... "A star" (*Persian*). A form of Esther. See also Hestia, below. DIM. Hetty.

Hestia .... In Greek mythology Hestia was the goddess of the hearth, or home, and her name was given to a star. Hestia may, therefore, also be a form of Hester, "a star" (*Persian*).

Hetty .... "A star" (*Persian*). A diminutive for both Hester and Esther.

WHAT SHALL WE NAME THE BABY?

Hilda .... "War maid" (*Teutonic*). In Norse mythology Hilda was one of the Valkyrs, maidens who bore the souls of slain warriors to Valhalla.

Hildegard, Hildegarde .... "Protecting battle-maid" (*Teutonic*).

Holly .... A name from the shrub. In olden days holly was hung inside a house at Christmastide as an evergreen winter refuge for the elves who were supposed to bring good luck in gratitude.

Honoria, Honora .... "Honor" (*Latin*). DIM. Nora, Norah.

Hope .... An Old English "virtue" name, a favorite with the Puritans.

Hortense .... "Worker in a garden, or gardener" (*Latin*).

Huberta .... "Bright-minded" (*Teutonic*). Feminine of Hubert.

Huette .... "Little Hugh," or "small intelligent girl" (*Teutonic*). A diminutive feminine of Hugh.

Hugette, Huguette .... A feminine diminutive of Hugh, like Huette, above.

Hulda, Huldah .... "A weasel or mole" (*Hebrew*). A Biblical prophetess.

Hypatia .... "Surpassing" (*Greek*). Figuratively "an intellectually superior woman," because of a 4th century teacher and philosopher of Alexandria, famous for her beauty and learning.

I

Ianthe .... A name coined by Lord Byron for the lady
to whom he dedicated his poem "Childe Harold."
In Greek it signifies a violet-colored flower.

Ida .... "Happy" (*Teutonic*).

Idalia .... Another name for Aphrodite, the Greek
Venus, so called from Idalia, a city in Cyprus
which was sacred to her.

Idaline, Idalina .... Either varied forms of Idalia, above;
or of Adalia, "noble" (*Teutonic*), or an elaborated
form of Ida, "happy" (*Teutonic*).

Idelle .... An elaborated form of Ida, "happy" (*Teutonic*).

Idette .... A diminutive form of Ida, above. The "ette"
means "little."

Idola .... "A vision" (*Greek*).

Idona .... "The industrious, or constant, worker" (*Teutonic*). The name comes from the Norse goddess
Iduna, who fed the gods with apples which kept
them immortal.

Ignacia, Ignatia .... "Ardent or fiery" (*Latin*). Feminine forms of Ignatius.

Ilka .... "Industrious" (*Teutonic-Latin*). A contraction
of Milka, a Slavonic form of Emily.

Imogene, Imogen .... Perhaps originally Imagina, meaning "image or likeness" (*Latin*). Made popular by
Shakespeare's heroine in "Cymbeline."

Ina .... Properly merely a feminine suffix, as in Paulina, Rosina, etc., but in recent years used as an
individual name.

Inez, Ines .... "Pure, gentle, meek" (*Greek*). Forms,
originally Spanish, of Agnes.

Inga .... "Daughter" (*Teutonic*). See Ingrid, below.

Ingrid .... "Ing" was a hero-god of Teutonic mythology, ancestor of the Danes and Swedes, and supposed founder of the line of Swedish kings. From
this Ing (whose name means merely "son") the

feminine Ingrid is derived, and so may be translated "daughter."

Iona .... Probably derived from the ancient Greek colony of Ionia, whence our Ionic architecture. But it may be from the Greek word meaning "a violet-colored precious stone."

Iphigenia .... In Greek mythology Iphigenia was a beautiful maiden offered as a sacrifice, but snatched from the altar by the goddess Artemis and carried to heaven.

Irene .... "Peace" (*Greek*). Irene, or Eirene, was the Greek goddess of peace.

Iris .... "The rainbow" (*Greek*). In Greek mythology Iris was the messenger of the gods. In the Bible narrative (Genesis ix) a rainbow was set in the clouds as a "covenant" to mark the ending of the Flood.

Irma .... A short form of Irmina, below.

Irmina .... "Noble" (*Latin*). Also sometimes used as short for Hermione, which see.

Isabel, Isabelle .... Forms of Isabella, below.

Isabella .... Although this name has long been considered another form of Elizabeth, and so to mean "consecrated to God" (*Hebrew*), it probably came originally from Jezebel, or "oath to Baal"—Baal being the "false god" of the Hebrews. DIM. Bell, Belle, Bella.

Isidora, Isadora .... Probably "gift of Isis" (*Greek*); but as Isis was the Egyptian goddess of the moon these names may signify "gift of the moon." Feminine forms of Isidore.

74

sleen .... A name of modern coinage, perhaps suggested by Eileen.

Isobel .... A Scotch form of Isabel, above.

Isolde, Isolda .... "The fair" (*Celtic*). In the King Arthur legends Isolde was a princess beloved by Tristan.

Iva .... A short form of Ivana, below.

Ivana, Ivane .... "God's gracious gift" (*Hebrew*). Feminines of Ivan, the Russian form of John.

Ivy .... A "plant" name from the clinging evergreen vine. The ivy was sacred to Aphrodite, the Greek goddess of love.

J

Jacinta .... Figuratively "lovely, beautiful" because of the flower hyacinth, from which the Greek name comes. In classical mythology the hyacinth is supposed to have sprung from the blood of a fair youth.

Jacoba, Jakoba .... Feminine forms, the latter German, of Jacob, which means "the supplanter" (*Hebrew*).

Jacqueline .... "The supplanter" (*Hebrew*). A feminine form, through the French Jacques, of Jacob or James.

Jane .... "God's gracious gift" (*Hebrew*). The usual feminine for John; but actually a contraction of Johanna, which see for diminutives.

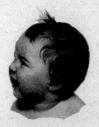

Janel, Janella .... Forms, probably of modern coinage, of Jane, above.

Janet, Janette, Janetta .... Diminutive forms of Jane, above.

Janice .... An elaborated form of Jane, above.

Jaquenette, Jaquenetta .... "The supplanter" (*Hebrew*). Feminine forms, through the French Jacques, of Jacob or James. The endings mean "little."

Jarita .... The name of a bird in Hindu legend. She so devotedly protected her offspring that she was given a human soul.

Jasmine .... A "flower" name from the fragrant blossom. Originally a Persian word.

Jean .... A Scotch form of Jane, above.

Jeanne .... A French form of Johanna or Joan. Jeanne d'Arc, "the maid of Orleans," is a French national heroine.

Jeannette .... A French diminutive form of Johanna or Jane.

Jemima .... "A dove" (*Hebrew*). A Biblical name.

Jennifer .... "White wave" (*Celtic*).

Jenny .... A diminutive of Jane or Johanna, which see.

Jessica .... Either "grace of God," or "rich" (*Hebrew*). An individual name; also the feminine of Jesse. DIM. Jessy, Jessie, Jess.

Jessie, Jessy .... Diminutives of Jessica, above.

Jewel .... "A jewel or gem" (*Latin*). It may also mean "delight." See Joy, below.

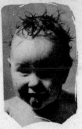

Jill .... Originally a short form of Julia; but in Old English usage also a nickname meaning merely "girl" or "sweetheart."

Joan .... "God's gracious gift" (*Hebrew*). Like Jane and Johanna, a feminine form of John.

Jobina, Jobyna .... Feminine forms of Job, which means "the persecuted" (*Hebrew*).

Jocelyn, Jocelin .... "Merry or jocund" (*Latin*).

Johanna "God's gracious gift" (*Hebrew*). Feminine of John. DIM. Joan, Jane, Jean, Janet, Jenny.

Josephine Feminine of Joseph, which means "He shall add" (*Hebrew*).

Joy "Delight" (*Old French*). The same word may also mean "jewel" from its Latin derivation.

Joyce .... "Joyful, rejoicing" (*Old French*).

Juanita .. A Spanish form of Johanna, above.

Judith "The praised" (*Hebrew*). DIM. Judy.

Juditha A Latin form of Judith, above.

Judy .... An abbreviation of Judith, above.

Julia .... Feminine of Julius, which see. The male name was made famous throughout the world by Julius Caesar. DIM. Juliet, Julie, Jill.

Juliana, Juliane .... Forms of Julia, above.

Julie .... A French form of Julia, above.

Julienne .. A French feminine form of Julian or Julius.

Juliet, Julietta .... Diminutives, for the last syllables mean "little," of Julia. The name Juliet was made popular in English by Shakespeare in "Romeo and Juliet."

Julita .... An abbreviation of Julietta, above.

June .... "Youthful" (*Latin*). A name from the month, which was called after the Roman family "Junius" meaning "the young."

Juno .... In Roman mythology the goddess Juno was queen of heaven, wife of Jupiter, and the special guardian of women.

Justine, Justina .... "The just or upright" (*Latin*). Feminine forms of Justin.

K

Kara .... "Pure" (*Greek*). An abbreviated form, through Karena, of Katharine.

Karen, Karin, Karena .... "Pure" (*Greek*). Shortened forms, the first Danish, of Katharine.

Kasia, Kassia .... "Pure" (*Greek*). Polish forms of Katharine.

Kate .... "Pure" (*Greek*). A short form of Katharine or Catherine, but also used as an independent name.

Katharine, Katherine, Kathryn .... "Pure" (*Greek*). Originally spelled with a "K" as in the Greek, these names have also come down to us as Catherine, etc., because there was no "K" in the Anglo-Saxon alphabet and "C" was substituted. For diminutives and variants see Catherine.

Kathie .... "Pure" (*Greek*). A diminutive of Katharine.

Kathleen .... "Pure" (*Greek*). An Irish endearing form of Katharine. But it may also be from the Celtic name of a star, meaning "beam of the wave."

Katrina, Katrine .... Forms of Katharine, above.

Kay .... "Exultant, or rejoicing" (*Greek*). Also used as a nickname for Katharine.

Kelda .... "A spring or fountain" (*Old Norse*).

Kendra .... "The knowing, or understanding" (*Anglo-Saxon*).

Kirstie .... "The Christian, or anointed" (*Greek*). A Scotch nickname for Christine or Christina.

Kit, Kittie .... Nicknames for Katharine or Catherine.

Koren .... "Maiden" (*Greek*).

L

Laïs .... A Greek name of obscure meaning. A favorite with the poets.

Lalage .... A name often used by ancient lyric poets. Literally it means "free of speech, or talkative" (*Greek*).

Lalita .... Perhaps "artless, straightforward" (*Sanskrit*); or it may come from the same Greek word as Lalage, above.

Lara .... "Famous" (*Latin*). In Latin mythology Lara was a nymph punished by Jove for her talkativeness.

Larentia .... In Latin mythology Larentia was the foster-mother of Romulus and Remus, founders of Rome.

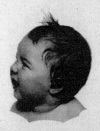

Larina, Larine .... "Sea gull" (*Latin*).

Larissa .... "Cheerful or laughing" (*Latin*).

Latona .... From Latonia, the Roman name of the Greek goddess Leto. She was mother of the sun-god Apollo and of the moon goddess Diana.

Laura .... "The laurel" (*Latin*)—the symbol of victory. The feminine of Lawrence, which see.

Laurel .... "The laurel" (*Latin*). See Lawrence.

Laurella .... A form of Laura, above.

Laurene, Laureen, Laurena .... "The laurel-crowned, or victorious" (*Latin*). Varied forms of Laura, which may be used as feminines of Lawrence.

Lauretta, Laurette .... Diminutives of Laura. The endings "etta" and "ette" mean "little."

Laurice, Loris .... "The laurel" (*Latin*). Feminine contractions of Lawrence.

Laverna .... The original bearer of this name was the ancient Latin goddess of profit or gain; but, if traced through the Old French, the name may also mean "vernal or springlike."

Lavinia, Lavina .... Lavinia was the daughter of King Latinus in Roman mythology. She is supposed to personify the Latin race.

Lea .... Either a contraction of Leah, "the weary" (*Hebrew*); or the feminine of Leo, and so meaning "lioness" (*Latin*).

Leah .... "The weary" (*Hebrew*). The Biblical Leah was the mother of six of the twelve Hebrew patriarchs.

Leila .... A Moorish name, first made popular by the heroine of Byron's poem "The Giaour," and later by Bulwer-Lytton in his novel "Leila."

Lelia, Lela, Lelah .... From Laelius, the name of a famous ancient Latin clan. Its significance is unexplained. In modern usage these names are often derived from Lilian.

Lemuela .... "Dedicated to God" (*Hebrew*). The feminine of Lemuel.

Lena, Lina .... "Light" (*Greek*). Originally diminutives of Helena; but now used also as diminutives of other names ending in "lena," "lina," or "line," such as Madelena, Evelina, Caroline, etc.

Lenita, Leneta .... "Gentle or mild" (*Latin*).

Leola .... Either a feminine of Leo; or, more probably, a contraction of the Italian Liliola, which comes not from Lilian but from Cecilia!

Leonie .... A French feminine form of Leon, which means "the lion" (*Latin*).

Leonora, Leonore, Lenora, Lenore .... "Light" (*Greek*). Forms of Eleonora. The name Lenore was made popular by Poe in his poem "The Raven."

Leontine .... "Lion-like" (*Latin*).

Leora .... "Light" (*Greek*). A contraction of Leonora.

Leslie, Lesley .... Feminine forms of the masculine "residence" name, Leslie, which means "from the gray fort" (*Celtic*).

Leta .... "Joy" (*Latin*). A diminutive of Letitia.

Lethia .... From the river Lethe in Greek mythology, the name of which means "forgetfulness" because its waters bestowed oblivion.

Letitia .... "Joy or gladness" (*Latin*). DIM. Letty, Leta.

Letty, Lettie .... "Joy or gladness" (*Latin*).

Lexine .... "Helper of mankind" (*Greek*). Short for Alexine, a feminine form of Alexander.

Liane, Liana .... "A bond or binding" (*French-Latin*).

Libby .... "Consecrated to God" (*Hebrew*). A diminutive of Elizabeth.

Lilia .... A form of Lilian, below.

Lilian, Lillian .... "A lily" (*Greek*). In ancient Egypt the lily was the symbol of life and resurrection. In modern usage it has become the symbol of purity from the white lily of the Annunciation. DIM. Lilly, Lily, Lil.

Lilis, Lillis .... Forms of Lilian. But the first form, Lilis, is also a variant of Lilith, below.

Lilith .... In the Jewish Talmud Lilith was the legendary wife of Adam before Eve. In folklore she took the form of a beautiful but snake-like woman who brought misfortune. She appeared only by night; and our "lullaby" was originally a chant to ward her off.

Lilla, Lila, Lilah .... "The lily" (*Greek*). Variants of Lilian. Formerly these names were also used as contractions of Elizabeth.

Lily, Lili .... Contractions of Lilian, above.

Lilybell .... "Fair Lily, or Lilian" (*Latin*). See Lilian, above.

Linda .... "Beautiful" (*Latin*).

Linette, Linnette, Lynette .... May mean either "graceful or shapely" (*Celtic*), or "the linnet," a "bird" name (*Anglo-Latin*), or "little lioness" (*French-Latin*). The story of Lynette of the King Arthur legends is told by Tennyson in "Gareth and Lynette."

Lisa, Liza .... "Consecrated to God" (*Hebrew*). Diminutives of Elizabeth.

Lisabetta, Lisabette, Lisabet .... "Consecrated to God" (*Hebrew*). Forms of Elizabeth.

Lise .... A German diminutive of Elizabeth, "consecrated to God" (*Hebrew*).

Lisette, Lisetta, Lizette, Lizetta .... "Consecrated to God" (*Hebrew*). Diminutive forms of Elizabeth. But in France Lisette is also used as a diminutive of Louise.

Livia .... Originally this name was made famous by Livia, the first Roman empress. Nowadays it is usually taken as a short form of Olivia, "the olive" (*Latin*).

Lizzie .... "Consecrated to God" (*Hebrew*). A diminutive of Elizabeth.

Loïs .... Originally a Greek name of unknown meaning; but nowadays usually considered a feminine of Louis, or a short form of Louisa.

Lola .... A Spanish diminutive of Charlotte, therefore a feminine of Charles.

Lolita, Loleta .... Elaborated forms of Lola, above.

Lona .... "The single, or alone" (*Middle English*).

WHAT SHALL WE NAME THE BABY?

Lorelei .... "A siren." In German folklore Lorelei wa
a siren of the Rhine who lured mariners to ship
wreck by her singing. Literally the name mean
"lurer to the rock" (*Old High German*).

Lorelle, Lorella, Lorilla .... "Little, or elfin, Laura
(*Latin-Teutonic*).

Lorena A feminine form of Lawrence, "the laurel
(*Latin*).

Loretta, Lorette .... "Small wise one" (*Anglo-Saxon*).

Lorinda A form (originally Latin) of Laura.

Lorita .... A diminutive of Laura, "the laurel" (*Latin*)

Lorna ... A short form of Lorena, above.

Lorraine, Loraine .... A "place" name from the Frencl
Duchy of Lorraine, which signifies "famous i
war" (*Old High German*). The name Louis ha
the same meaning.

Lotta, Lotty, Lottie .... Diminutives of Charlotte. Th
first is a Swedish form.

Lotus .... A "flower" name from the sacred Egyptia
lotus, or lily of the Nile. In Homer's "Odyssey'
the fruit of the lotus tree produced dreamy forget
fulness.

Lou ... A diminutive of Louisa, below.

Louisa, Louise "Famous in battle" (*Teutonic*). Fem
inines of Louis. VARIANTS AND DIMINUTIVES: He
loïse, Lisette, Loïs, Lulu, Lou.

Lucia .... "Light" (*Latin*). An Italian and Spanish forn
of Lucy.

Luciana .... "Light" (*Latin*). An Italian variant of Lucy

Lucie .... "Light" (*Latin*). A French form of Lucy.

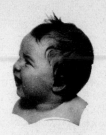

Lucilla .... "Light" (*Latin*). A variant of Lucy.

Lucille .. "Light" (*Latin*). A French form of Lucy.

Lucina .... Lucina was the Roman goddess of childbirth. Her name means "light."

Lucinda .... "Light" (*Latin*). A variant of Lucy.

Lucrèce ... "Bringer of light" (*Latin*). A French form of Lucretia, below.

Lucretia .... "Bringer of light" (*Latin*). The origin of this name is probably Lucifer, meaning "the light-bringer." But it may also spring from another Latin word meaning "gain." The Lucretia of Roman legend was famous for her wifely virtue.

Lucy .... "Light" (*Latin*). A favorite name for a child born at daybreak. The feminine of Lucius.

Luella, Louella .... If from the Latin these names mean "expiation." In modern use they may be a combination of Louis and Ella.

Lulita .... Probably a "pet," or diminutive, form of Louisa.

Lulu .... A "pet," or diminutive, form of Louisa.

Luna .... "Shining" (*Latin*). The name of the Roman goddess of the moon.

Lurline .... A variant of Lorelei, which see.

Lydia .... "From Lydia" (*Greek*). Lydia was an ancient province of Asia Minor, whose inhabitants were noted for their culture.

Lynn, Lynna .... "A cascade" (*Anglo-Saxon*).

Lyris .... From the Greek word for "lyre," or harp, so suggesting melody and song.

M

Mabel, Mabelle .... "Amiable, loveable" (*Latin*). Originally shortened forms of Amabel.

Madel, Maidel .... Shortened forms, through Madeleine of Magdelen, which means "the tower" (*Hebrew*)

Madeleine, Madelaine, Madelene, Madeline, Madelena, Madalyn .... "The tower" (*Hebrew*). Forms o Magdalen. DIM. Madel, Maidel.

Madelon .... A popular French form of Magdalen below.

Madge .... "A pearl" (*Greek*). A short form of Mar garet.

Madra .... An English spelling of "madre," the Italian for "mother."

Mae .... Another spelling of May, which see.

Magdala .... "A tower" (*Hebrew*). See Magdalen below.

Magdalen, Magdalene, Magdalena .... The Biblical Mary Magdalene was so called frcm Magdala, the tow from which she came. It means "a tower" (*Hebrew*) because of a watch-tower, the ruins o which still remain. The two last forms are German and Spanish, respectively.

Maggie .... "A pearl" (*Greek*). A diminutive, originally Scotch, of Margaret.

Magnolia .... From the magnolia, a tree with fragran flowers, named for the French botanist Magnol.

Maia, Maya .... In Latin mythology, Maia, from whom our month of May was named, was the goddess of growth or spring. It is also a star name, Maia being one of the brightest of the Pleiades.

Maida, Mayda .... "A maiden" (*Anglo-Saxon*).

Maire, Mair .... Irish and Welsh forms of Mary, which see.

Maisie .... "A pearl" (*Greek*). A Scotch abbreviation of Margaret.

Malina .... "A tower" (*Hebrew*). A form of Magdalen, through its Danish abbreviation, Malin.

Malva .... "Soft" (*Greek*). A "flower" name from the mallow.

Manda .... "Loveable" (*Latin*). An abbreviation of Amanda.

Manette .... A diminutive of Manon, below.

Manon .... A French abbreviation, through Marion, of Mary.

Manuela .... "God with us" (*Hebrew*). The feminine of Manuel.

Mara .... The original Hebrew form of Mary. (See Ruth i:20.)

Maraline .... An elaborated form of Mary.

Marcella, Marcelle .... Short forms of Marcellina and Marcelline, below.

Marcellina, Marcelline .... Feminine forms, through Marcellus, of Marcus or Mark, which see.

Marcia .... The feminine of Marcus, or Mark, which see.

Marea .... Either "of the sea" (*Latin*), or a varie
spelling of Maria.

Marelda .... "Famous battle-maid" (*Teutonic*).

Marella .... "Little Mary," or "elfin Mary."

Maretta, Marette .... Shorter forms of Marietta an
Mariette, below.

Margalo, Margolo .... Forms of Margaret, below.

Margaret .... "A pearl" (*Greek*). The original Persia
word from which the Greek name is derived migh
be translated "born of moonlight," from th
fancy that pearls were created from dewdrop
which pearl-oysters, rising from the sea, receive
on moonlit nights. DIMINUTIVES AND VARIANTS
Margery, Marjorie, Margot, Madge, Maisie, Mag
gie, Mag, Meg, Peggy, Peg, Meta, Rita, Daisy
Gretchen, Gredel, Greta.

Margarita, Margareta, Margaretta .... Varied forms o
Margaret, above.

Margot .... A French diminutive of Margaret, made
popular in France by Margaret of Valois, "la
reine Margot" of history and romance.

Marguerite .... A form of Margaret, above. In French
"marguerite" means both "pearl" and the flowe
"daisy," which accounts for Daisy as a nickname
for Margaret. The flower was probably so called
from its whiteness.

Maria, Marya The first originally the Latin, the
second a Polish, form of Mary.

Mariamne .... "Rebellious" (*Hebrew*). A form o
Miriam, which see.

Marian, Marion .... Forms, originally Old French, o
Mary.

Marianna, Mariana, Marianne .... A combination o
Mary and Anne— the names of the Virgin Mary
and of her mother. Marianne, the French form, has
come to symbolize modern France much as "Uncle
Sam" does America.

Maribel .... "Mary the beautiful" (*Hebrew-Latin*).

Marice .... A form of Mary.

Marie .... The standard French form of Mary.

Mariel .... A Bavarian form of Mary.

Marietta, Mariette .... Italian and French diminutives of Mary.

Marigold .... A name from the golden-yellow flower, marigold, originally called "Mary's gold."

Marilla .... An elaborated form of Mary.

Marilyn, Marylyn .... Elaborated forms of Mary.

Marina .... "Maid of the sea" (*Latin*).

Marjorie, Marjory, Margery .... "A pearl" (*Greek*). Variants, the first originally Scotch, of Margaret.

Marla .... A Bavarian form of Mary.

Marlene, Marlena .... "The tower" (*Hebrew*). Forms of Magdalen.

Marnia .... A variation of Marina, meaning "maid of the sea" (*Latin*).

Marta .... "Lady, or mistress" (*Aramean*). A short form of Martha.

Martella .... Either a form of Martina, below, or a diminutive of Martha.

Martha .... "Lady, or mistress" (*Aramean*). The Biblical Martha (Luke x:41) has become the patron saint of careful housewives. DIM. Marta, Mattie, Matty, Patty.

Martina, Martine .... "Martial, warlike" (*Latin*). Feminine forms of Martin.

WHAT SHALL WE NAME THE BABY?

Mary .... In commemoration of the Virgin Mary, this
has become the most frequently bestowed name in
all Christian countries. During the Middle Ages it
was sometimes translated as "Star of the Sea"
(*Latin*); but its true meaning—now long since
lost—is undoubtedly "bitter" (*Hebrew*). The
name originates in the Biblical Book of Ruth
(i:20) where Naomi cries, "Call me not Naomi
[pleasantness], call me Mara [bitter]: for the Al-
mighty hath dealt very bitterly with me." DIMIN-
UTIVES AND VARIANTS: Maria, Mara, Marea,
Marya, Marie, Marian, Mariel, Marla, Marella,
Marilla, Maraline, Marilyn, Marietta, Mariette,
Marice, Manon, Manette, Moya, Moira, Maire,
May, Mae, Minnie, Molly, Polly.

Maryann, Mary Ann .... Mary and Ann combined.

Matilda, Mathilda, Mathilde .... "Mighty in battle"
(*Teutonic*). A name first brought to England by
the wife of William the Conqueror (1066). DIM.
Tilda, Tilly, Matty, Mattie, Maud, Maude.

Matty, Mattie .... Diminutives either of Matilda or of
Martha.

Maud, Maude .... "Mighty in battle" (*Teutonic*). Now
used as independent names, but originally contractions of Matilda.

Maura, Maure .... "Dark" (*Latin*). Feminine forms of
Maurice. If from the Celtic they may also mean
"great."

Maurella .... "Dark and elfin" (*Latin-Teutonic*).

Maurine, Maureen .... "The dark" (*Latin*). Usually Irish names, which, if taken from the Celtic, may also signify "great."

Maurita .... "Dark" (*Latin*).

Mavia .... Either a form of Mavis, below; or from another old Celtic word which means "joy, or mirth."

Mavis .... "The song-thrush" (*Celtic*). A "bird" name.

Mavra .... A Russian form of Maura, meaning "dark" (*Latin*).

Maxine, Maxime .... "The greatest" (*Latin*). Feminine forms of Maximilian.

May .... Though so short a name this may be interpreted in an unusual number of ways: (1) from the spring month, (2) from Maia, the Latin goddess of growth, (3) "kinswoman" (*Anglo-Saxon*), (4) "maiden" (*Middle English*), (5) an abbreviation of Mary.

Medea .... The name of a famous sorceress in Greek mythology. It may mean "ruler" (*Greek*).

Medora .... A name probably coined by Lord Byron in his poem "The Corsair" (1814), where Medora figures as the corsair's patient wife.

Meg .... "A pearl" (*Greek*). A Scotch nickname for Margaret.

Megan .... "The strong or able" (*Anglo-Saxon*).

Mehetabel, Mehitabel .... "Favored by God" (*Hebrew*).

Melanie, Melania .... In Greek mythology Melania was the name given to Demeter, the earth goddess, when mourning during the winter for her daughter Persephone, the spring. It means "darkness, or clad in black" (*Greek*).

Melantha .... "Dark flower" (*Greek*).

Melissa, Melisse .... "The honey-bee, or honey" (*Greek*). In classic mythology Melissa was a nymph who first taught men the use of honey.

Melita, Melleta .... "Honey-sweet" (*Greek*). See Melissa, above.

Melva .... A contraction of Melvina, below.

Melvina, Malvina .... Either "handmaiden" or "chieftainess" (*Celtic*). This is a seeming contradiction, but the root-word may signify both "servant" and "master." Feminines of Malvin.

Mercedes .... "The rewarding or favoring." From the Spanish title of the Virgin as "Maria de Mercedes."

Mercia .... "From Mercia." Mercia was an ancient Anglo-Saxon kingdom on the Welsh border. A "place" name.

Mercy .... "The merciful or compassionate" (*French-Latin*). A "virtue" name.

Meris .... "Of the sea, or sea-born" (*Latin*). Originally Maris.

Merle .... "A blackbird" (*Latin*).

Meryl, Meriel .... "Myrrh" (*Arabic*). Variants of Muriel, which see.

Meta .... Usually a diminutive of Margaret, "a pearl" (*Greek*); but may also be short for Almeta, "ambitious" (*Latin*).

Mettabel .... "Favored by God" (*Hebrew*). A form of Mehetabel.

Mignon .... "Dainty" or "a favorite or darling" (*Old French*). A name made popular by Goethe's heroine in "Wilhelm Meister" (1795).

Mildred .... "Mild, or gentle, counselor" (*Anglo-Saxon*).

Milicent, Millicent, Melicent .... "Strength" (*Teutonic*). If taken from a more modern origin these names may signify "thousand saints" or "mille sanctis" (*Old French-Latin*).

Milly, Millie .... Now used as individual names, though originally contractions of Milicent and Mildred, above.

Mimi ... A French diminutive form of Wilhelmina.

Minerva .... Symbolizing "wisdom," from Minerva, the Roman goddess of wisdom. The name literally means "mind" (*Greek*).

Minna .... "Remembrance, or loving memory" (*Teutonic*). Also a diminutive of Wilhelmina.

Minnie, Minny .... Nowadays commonly used as diminutives of Mary; but originally meaning "remembrance, or loving memory" (*Teutonic*).

Mirabelle .... "Of wondrous beauty" (*Latin-French*). A name probably coined by Edmund Spenser in his "Faerie Queene" (1590).

Miranda .... "Deserving of admiration" (*Latin*). The heroine of Shakespeare's "The Tempest."

Miriam .... "Rebellious" (*Hebrew*). In the Old Testament narrative, Miriam and her brother Aaron joined in complaint against Moses; and her name literally means "their rebellion." But some authorities consider it a form of Mary.

Moina, Moyna .... "Gentle or soft" (*Celtic*).

Moira .... "The great" (*Celtic*). Also used in Ireland as a variant of Mary.

Molly, Mollie .... Diminutives of Mary.

Mona .... "The single or solitary" (*Teutonic-Latin*).

Monica A name of uncertain origin. Perhaps meaning "adviser" (*Latin*); perhaps a contraction of Dominica, which see.

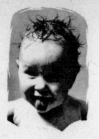

Moria .... A name probably coined by Ben Jonson in his "Cynthia's Revels" (1601).

Morna .... "Gentle" (*Celtic*). Morna was the daughter of an ancient Irish king whose tragic story survives in Celtic folklore.

Moya .... "The great" (*Celtic*). A variant of Moira. Also used in Ireland as a form of Mary.

Muriel .... "Myrrh" (*Arabic*). Myrrh is a fragrant gum, once so highly prized that, like gold and frank-incense, it was presented by the Wise Men to the Christ Child. Like "Mary," the word in Hebrew means "bitter" from the bitter taste of myrrh.

Myra, Mira .... "The wonderful" (*Latin*).

Myrilla, Mirilla .... Elaborated forms of Myra, above.

Myrta, Merta .... Forms of Myrtle, below.

Myrtle .... "The myrtle" (*Greek*). A name from the evergreen shrub or tree. In ancient Greece the myrtle was highly esteemed as sacred to Venus, and its leaves were used for crowns of victory.

N

Nada .... "Hope" (*Slavonic*). In Russian Nada is the Hope of the three holy virtues, Faith, Hope and Charity.

Nadine .... A French form of Nada, above.

Nan .... "Grace" (*Hebrew*). A diminutive of Hannah or Ann.

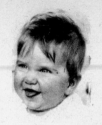

Nana, Nanna .... "Grace" (*Hebrew*). Diminutives of Hannah or Ann.

Nancy .... "Grace" (*Hebrew*). A diminutive of Hannah or Ann, but also used as an independent name.

Nanelle, Nanelia .... Variants of Nan, above.

Nanette, Nanetta .... Variants of Nan, above.

Nanine .... A variant of Nan, above.

Nanny, Nannie .... Variants of Nan, above.

Naomi .... "Sweet or pleasant" (*Hebrew*). A Biblical name.

Nara .... Perhaps from a Gaelic word meaning "happy."

Narda .... "The anointed" (*Persian*). "Nard" is the precious and fragrant ointment now called spikenard.

Natala, Natalia .... Forms, the second Italian and Spanish, of Natalie, below.

Natalie, Nathalie .... "Christmas child." Names derived from the Latin "dies natalis" or "birthday of our Lord," and often given to girls born at Christmastide. DIM. Netty.

Natasha, Natascha .... Russian forms of Natalie, above.

Nathania .... "Gift of the Lord" (*Hebrew*). The feminine of Nathaniel or Nathan.

Natica .... A short form of the Russian Natascha, meaning "Christmas child" (*Latin*).

Neala .... "Chieftainess" (*Celtic*). The feminine of Neal.

Neda .... "Sunday's child" (*Slavonic*).

Nedda .... A feminine diminutive form of Edward, meaning "prosperous guardian" (*Anglo-Saxon*).

Nelda .... Perhaps from the Old English "residence" surname, meaning "at the elder tree."

Nelia .... A short form of Cornelia, and so a feminine of Cornelius, which see.

Nell, Nelly, Nellie .... "Light" (*Greek*). Diminutives of Helen.

Nella .... A form of Nell, above.

Nellis .... A modern variant of Nell, above.

Nelma .... A variant of Nell, above.

Neoma .... "New moon" (*Greek*). A contraction of Neomenia, which was an ancient festival held at the time of the new moon. Daughters born under a new moon were often so named.

Nerine .... "A nereid," or nymph of the sea (*Greek*). In classical mythology the Nereids, daughters of the sea god Nereus, were beautiful maidens helpful to mariners.

Nerissa .... "Of the sea" (*Greek*).

Nerita .... "Of the sea" (*Greek*).

Nessa, Nessia .... "Pure" (*Greek*). Contractions of Agnessa, a Russian form of Agnes.

Netty, Nettie .... "Neat, well-shaped, tidy" (*Teutonic*). Also diminutives of Natalie.

Nevada .... "Snowy" (*Latin*). The state of Nevada was so named from its snow-capped mountains.

Neysa .... "Pure" (*Greek*). Another spelling of Neza, a Slavonic form of Agnes.

Nicolette .... "Little Nicholas." A feminine diminutive of Nicholas, which means "victory of the people" (*Greek*).

Nina .... "Grace" (*Hebrew*). A form of Nan or Ann. Nina in Spanish merely means "little girl."

Ninette "Little Nan, or Ann," a French diminutive.

Ninon, Nanon .... "Grace" (*Hebrew*). French diminutives of Ann.

Noel, Noelle, Noella .... "Christmas, or Christmasborn" (*French-Latin*). Noel is a French contraction of the Latin "natalis" in "dies natalis," referring to the birthday of Christ, or Christmas. It also means a Christmas carol, or song of joy.

Nola .... Either "noble, or famous" (*Celtic*) as the feminine of Nolan; or "the olive" (*Latin*) as the feminine of Oliver through its nickname Noll.

Noleta .... "The unwilling" (*Latin*).

Nolita .... "The olive" (*Latin*). A feminine diminutive of Oliver through its nickname Noll. See Oliver.

Nona .... "The ninth" (*Latin*). A name sometimes given to a ninth child, if a girl. In Latin mythology Nona was that one of the three Fates who spun the thread of life.

Norah, Nora .... Properly short forms of Honoria, meaning "honor" (*Latin*); but also used as diminutives of Eleanor or Leonora, meaning "light" (*Greek*).

Norine, Norina .... Contractions of Honoria, meaning "honor" (*Latin*).

Norma .... "The model or pattern" (*Latin*).

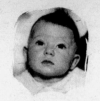

Nunciata .... "The messenger, or bearer of news" (*Latin*). A shorter form of Annunciata.

Nydia .... "A nest or refuge" (*Latin*). A name made popular by the heroine of Bulwer-Lytton's "Last Days of Pompeii."

O

Octavia .... "The eighth" (*Latin*). Feminine of Octavius.

Odelet, Odelette .... "Little song" (*French-Greek*).

Odelia, Odila .... "Wealthy or prosperous" (*Teutonic*).

Odile .... "Wealthy or prosperous" (*Teutonic*).

Ola .... Originally the feminine of Olaf, which see.

Olethea .... A name of modern coinage, perhaps a varied spelling of Alethea, meaning "truth" (*Latin*).

Olga .... "Holy" (*Teutonic*).

Olive .... "The olive" (*Latin*). Feminine for Oliver, which see for the symbolic meaning.

Olivia .... "The olive" (*Latin*). Feminine for Oliver, which see.

Opal .... A "gem" name. The opal, which in Sanskrit means "precious stone," was anciently believed to have magical powers, such as conferring invisibility, etc.

Ophelia .... A name made famous by Shakespeare in "Hamlet." It may come from the Greek word meaning "serpent," but the serpent in ancient days symbolized immortality and wisdom.

Ora .... Possibly a short form for any female name ending in "ora," like Honora, Eleonora, etc. But it may be interpreted as "pray," or "seacoast" (*Latin*), or "money" (*Anglo-Saxon*).

Oralia, Oralie .... Names of modern coinage possibly suggested by Aurelia, "the golden" (*Latin*).

Oriana .... "The golden" (*Latin*). A name coined by poets in the seventeenth century to celebrate Queen Elizabeth of England. If derived from the Celtic it may also mean "of white skin" or "fair."

Oribel .... A name of modern coinage. It may be translated as "golden beauty" (*Latin*).

Oriel .... "The golden" (*Old French-Latin*). A "bird" name from the oriole, or golden thrush.

Orlantha .... "Fame of the land" (*Teutonic*). The feminine of Orlando.

Orlena, Orlene .... "The golden" (*Latin*). The French city of Orléans (and so our New Orleans) was named from the Roman Emperor Aurelian whose name meant "the golden."

Ortrud, Ortrude .... Literally "serpent-maid" (*Teutonic*); but the serpent was anciently regarded as wise and graceful.

Orva .... Either "of golden worth" (*Old French*), or the feminine of Orvin, meaning "courageous friend" (*Anglo-Saxon*).

Ottilie, Ottillia .... "Fortunate battle-maid" (*Teutonic*).

Ouida .... A pseudonym coined from her first name by the popular nineteenth-century novelist, Louisa de la Ramée.

WHAT SHALL WE NAME THE BABY?

P

Pamela .... A name probably coined by Sir Philip Sidney in his "Arcadia" (1590), and later made fashionable by Richardson in his romantic novel "Pamela, or Virtue Rewarded." It has no historic meaning.

Pandora .... "The all-gifted" (*Greek*). In classic mythology Pandora was the first woman, and brought to earth a sealed box containing all the gifts of the gods to mankind. But when she opened it, all except "hope" took flight.

Pansy .... "A thought, or remembrance" (*Old French-Greek*). A "flower" name from the pansy or heart's-ease.

Panthea .... "Of all the gods" (*Greek*). The Pantheon was a Roman temple dedicated to all the divinities.

Parthenia .... "The maidenly or virginal" (*Greek*). From the title of the Greek goddess Athene Parthenos, or "Athene the virgin."

Patience .... "The patient." A "virtue" name.

Patricia .... "Noble, or well-born" (*Latin*). The feminine of Patrick. DIM. Pat, Patty, Patsy.

Patty .... A nickname for Patricia, above. Also a nickname, through Mattie, of Martha, "lady, or mistress" (*Aramean*).

Paula .... "Little" (*Latin*). A feminine form of Paul.

Paulette .... "Little" (*Latin*). A French feminine diminutive of Paul.

Pauline, Paulina .... "Little" (*Latin*). Feminines of Paul.

Paulita .... "Little" (*Latin*). A feminine diminutive of Paul.

Peace .... "The peaceful." A "virtue" name, favorite with the Puritans.

Pearl .... "The pearl." A "gem" name. The Latin word for pearl means "pear," because many pearls are pear-shaped.

Peggy, Peg .... "A pearl" (*Greek*). Diminutives, through Meg, of Margaret.

Penelope .... "The weaver" (*Greek*). The name has come to typify a faithful wife because of the Penelope in the Homeric legend, who, beset by lovers during her husband's absence, postponed their advances till she had finished a piece of weaving, but undid by night what she wove by day.

Penthea .... "The fifth" (*Greek*). A name sometimes bestowed upon a fifth child, if a girl.

Peony .... A "flower" name. The peony was named from Pæon, another title for Apollo as the Greek god of healing, because it was supposed to possess medicinal qualities.

Pepita .... A Spanish feminine diminutive of Joseph, which means "He shall add" (*Hebrew*). Here are its travels—Josephus, Giuseppe, Beppo, Peppo, Pepita!

Perdita .... "The lost" (*Latin*). A name made popular in English by the Perdita of Shakespeare's "The Winter's Tale."

Persis .... "Woman from Persia" (*Greek*). A favorite Puritan name because of the Biblical Persis whom St. Paul commended for her good works (Romans xvi:12).

Petrina .... A feminine form of Peter, meaning "a rock" (*Greek*).

Philana .... "Lover of mankind" (*Greek*). A feminine contraction of Philander.

Philippa .... "Lover of horses" (*Greek*). The feminine of Philip.

Phillida .... "The loving" (*Greek*). Like Phyllis, a favorite name with poets for a rustic maiden.

Phillina, Philina .... "The loving" (*Greek*).

Philomela, Philomel .... "The nightingale," which means "lover of the moon" (*Greek*). In Greek mythology Philomela was a maiden changed into a nightingale.

Philomena .... Either another form of Philomela, above; or a feminine of Philander, "lover of mankind" (*Greek*), through the Italian form Filomena.

Phoebe, Phebe .... "The shining or brilliant" (*Greek*). A special title given to the Greek goddess Artemis as goddess of the moon.

Phyllis, Phillis .... "A green bough" (*Greek*). In Greek mythology the maiden Phyllis, when deserted by her lover, was changed into a bare almond tree which leaved and blossomed again on his return. A favorite name with poets for a country maid.

Pierrette .... A French feminine diminutive, through Pierre, of Peter, "a rock" (*Greek*).

Pippa .... An Italian feminine diminutive of Philip, which means "lover of horses" (*Greek*).

Placida, Placidia .... "The serene or calm" (*Latin*).

Polly .... A familiar nickname, through Molly, for Mary.

Pollyanna .... A modern compound of Polly and Anna.

Pomona .... "Fruitful" (*Latin*). Pomona was the Latin goddess of fruits.

Poppy .... A "flower" name (*Old English-Latin*).

Portia .... A name popularized in English by Shakespeare's heroine in "The Merchant of Venice." It comes from the title of an ancient Roman clan, the Porcii, called "pig men," probably because their ancestors were swineherds.

Prima .... "The first," or first-born (*Latin*).

Primalia .... "The first" (*Latin*).

Primavera .... "Spring's beginning" (*Latin*).

Primrose .... "First rose" (*Latin*). A "flower" name.
The primrose was so called from its early blos-
soming and likeness to the wild rose in form.

Priscilla .... Literally "the ancient" (*Latin*). A name
derived from the title of a Latin clan, so called
from its great antiquity. The Biblical Priscilla,
"helper" of the Apostle Paul, accounts for the
popularity of this name.

Prudence .... "The prudent." A "virtue" name.

Prunella .... A "color" name, from the color of the
plum or prune (*Old French-Latin*).

Psyche .... "The spirit or soul" (*Greek*). In Greek
mythology Psyche was a maiden beloved by Cupid
but forbidden to behold him.

Q

Queena, Queeny, Queenie .... "A queen." But the old
Teutonic word from which "queen" is derived
meant merely "wife" or "woman."

Quenby .... "Womanly" (*Scandinavian*).

Quintina .... "The fifth" (*Latin*). A name sometimes
given to a fifth child, if a girl, as Quentin is used
for a boy.

R

Rachel .... "Ewe" (*Hebrew*)—and so, like Agnes, "the
lamb," significant of gentle innocence. DIM. Ray,
Rae.

Raïna .... Either "the mighty" (*Teutonic*), or "queen"
(*French-Latin*).

Ramona .... "Wise protectress" (*Teutonic*). Feminine
of Raymond. A name popularized in America by
Helen Hunt Jackson's novel "Ramona" (1884).

Rana, Rania .... "Royal" (*Sanskrit*). In Norse mythology Rana was the goddess of the sea.

Raphaela, Rafaela .... "Divine healer" (*Hebrew*). Feminine forms of Raphael.

Ray, Rae .... Usually nicknames for Rachel; but they may also mean "roe, or female deer" (*Scandinavian*).

Reba .... A short form of Rebecca, below.

Rebecca, Rebekah .... "The ensnarer" (*Hebrew*). A Bible name meaning literally "cord with a noose," and so signifying either a snare, or a firm binding, like the marriage troth. DIM. Becky, Reba.

Regina .... "Queen, or queenly" (*Latin*). The name also commemorates the Virgin Mary as Queen of Heaven.

Renata .... "Reborn" (*Italian-Latin*). A name of curious history. Ragnar, "warrior of judgment" (*Teutonic*), was a famous Danish chieftain whose kin ravaged Paris and invaded England. His name spread into Italy, where it became Renata and was retranslated as "reborn" (*Latin*)—a meaning it has since retained. In France it was contracted to Renée.

Renée .... See Renata, above.

Renita .... "Firm, self-poised" (*Latin*).

Reseda .... "Healing" (*Latin*). Reseda is the Latin name for the flower mignonette.

Rhea .... In Greek mythology Rhea was the daughter of Heaven and Earth and mother of the gods.

Rhoda .... "A rose" (*Greek*).

Ricarda .... "Powerful ruler" (*Teutonic*). An Italian feminine form of Richard.

Rita .... "A pearl" (*Greek*). A diminutive of Margarita or Margaret. Also used as an independent name.

Roberta .... "Of shining fame" (*Teutonic*). The feminine of Robert.

Robina .... "Of shining fame" (*Teutonic*). A feminine of Robin or Robert.

Robinette .... A French feminine diminutive of Robin or Robert, meaning "of shining fame" (*Teutonic*).

Roderica .... "Famous ruler or princess" (*Teutonic*). Feminine of Roderick.

Rolanda .... "Fame of the land" (*Teutonic*). Feminine of Roland.

Romilda, Romelda .... "Glorious battle-maid" (*Teutonic*).

Romola .... "The Roman" (*Latin*). "Rome" merely means "strong." This Italian name was made popular in English by George Eliot's novel "Romola."

Ronalda .... "Of mighty power" (*Teutonic*). Feminine of Ronald.

Rosa .... "A rose" (*Latin*). This was the original form of the name Rose.

Rosabel, Rosabelle, Rosabella .... "Beautiful rose" (*Latin*).

Rosalba .... "White rose" (*Latin*).

Rosalia, Rozalia .... Forms of Rose, below. Rosalia may also signify "a melody or tune" (*Italian*).

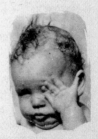

Rosalie .... A variant of Rose, below.

Rosalind, Rosalinde .... "Fair rose" (*Spanish-Latin*). The "lind" termination in Spanish means "fair."

Rosaline, Rosaleen, Rosalyn .... Elaborated forms of Rose, below.

Rosamond, Rosamund .... "Rose of the world" (*Latin*). This is the usual modern translation; but the original Teutonic name meant either "famed protector" or "protector of the horse"—the horse being the national emblem of the ancient Saxons.

Rosanna, Rosanne .... A combination of Rose and Anna, which may therefore be interpreted as "rose of grace" (*Latin-Hebrew*).

Rose .... "A rose" (*Latin*). A "flower" name, favorite in all languages.

Rosel, Roselle .... Diminutive variants, the first Swiss, of Rose, above.

Rosemarie .... A French form of Rosemary, below.

Rosemary .... Either "Mary's rose" (*Latin-Hebrew*), or "dew of the sea" (*Latin*). The flower rosemary is an emblem of remembrance.

Rosetta .... "Little Rose." An Italian diminutive.

Rosina, Rozina .... Variants of Rose, above.

Rowena .... "White mane" (*Celtic*). Rowena was a legendary Saxon princess, called "white mane" because the horse was the national emblem of the ancient Saxons. Sir Walter Scott revived the popularity of the name by making Rowena the heroine of his novel "Ivanhoe" (1819).

Roxana, Roxane .... "Dawn of day" (*Persian*). The latter is a French form.

Rubetta .... A diminutive of Ruby, below.

Ruby .... A "jewel" name from the most valuable of all the precious stones. The word merely means "red" (*Latin*).

Rue .... A "plant" name (*Greek*). The rue was formerly called "the herb of grace" because it was used to sprinkle holy water upon a penitent.

Ruth .... Either "a friend" or "beauty" (*Hebrew*). The story of the Biblical Ruth is vividly told in the Old Testament book that bears her name.

S

Sabine, Sabina .... "A Sabine"—that is, from the ancient Italian tribe of the Sabines. The meaning of the name is lost. The famous Poppæa Sabina was a Roman empress celebrated for her beauty and extravagance, who bathed in milk and shod her mules with gold.

Sabrina .... Sabrina was a legendary English princess drowned in the River Severn. The Romans called it by her name. She figures in Milton's "Comus."

Sacha .... "Helper of mankind" (*Greek*). A Russian feminine form of Alexander.

Sadie .... "Princess" (*Hebrew*). A diminutive of Sarah.

WHAT SHALL WE NAME THE BABY?

Sadira .... The old Arabic name for a constellation. Literally translated it means "ostrich returning from water."

Sally, Sallie .... "Princess" (*Hebrew*). Diminutives of Sarah.

Salome .... "Peaceful" (*Hebrew*).

Samala .... "Asked of God" (*Hebrew*). A contraction of Samuela, below.

Samara .... "From Samaria," the ancient city in Palestine. Samaria means "watch, or outlook, mountain" (*Hebrew*).

Samuela .... "Asked of God" (*Hebrew*). Feminine of Samuel.

Sandra .... "Helper of mankind" (*Greek*). A feminine diminutive of Alexander.

Sapphira .... Either "the beautiful" (*Hebrew*); or, if from the Greek, "the sapphire"—a "jewel" name.

Sarah, Sara .... "Princess" (*Hebrew*). The original name of the Biblical Sarah, wife of Abraham, was Sarai, "the contentious," but this was changed to Sarah, "princess," that she might become the mother of princes. DIM. Sally, Sadie.

Sarita .... "Little princess." A variant of Sarah.

Savina .... A varied spelling of Sabina, which see.

Secunda .... "The second" (*Latin*).

Sela .... "A rock" (*Hebrew*).

Selene, Selena .... "The moon" (*Greek*). In Greek mythology Selene was the goddess of the moon.

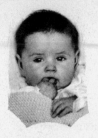 

Seleta .... "A rock" (*Hebrew*). A form of Sela.

Selima .... "Peaceful" (*Hebrew*). An Arabic feminine form of Solomon.

Selma .... Either "fair" (*Celtic*), or a feminine contraction of Anselm which means "divine helmet" (*Teutonic*).

Senalda .... "A sign, or signal" (*Spanish*).

Septima .... "The seventh" (*Latin*). A name sometimes given to a seventh child, if a daughter; or to a girl born in September. September was so called because it was the seventh month of the Roman year.

Seraphine, Serafine, Serafina .... "The burning or ardent" (*Hebrew*). A Seraph was a Biblical angel of the highest rank, distinguished for religious ardor.

Serena .... "The serene, or tranquil" (*Latin*).

Serilda .... "Armored warrior-maid" (*Teutonic*).

Sheila, Sheelah .... Irish forms of Cecilia, which see.

Shirley .... Originally an Old English "residence" surname, meaning "from the white meadow." Made popular by the heroine of Charlotte Brontë's novel "Shirley" (1849).

Sibley .... Either derived from Sibyl, below; or from the Anglo-Saxon, meaning "the related or friendly."

Sibyl, Sybil .... "Wise, or prophetic" (*Greek*). The ancient Sibyls of Roman mythology were supposed to prophesy under divine inspiration.

Sibylla, Sybilla .... Forms of Sibyl, above.

Sidonia, Sidonie .... A name derived from the ancient Phoenician seaport Sidon, which in Hebrew signifies "to ensnare." Compare the male name Sidney.

Sidra .... "Starlike" (*Latin*).

Silva .... "Woodland maid" (*Latin*). A contraction of Sylvia.

Silver .... A name from the precious metal. In Anglo-Saxon the word means "white."

Simona .... "Heard" (*Hebrew*). Feminine of Simon.

Sirena .... "A siren" (*Greek*).

Solita .... "The wonted, or accustomed" (*Latin*).

Sonia, Sonya .... Slavonic forms of Sophia, below.

Sophia, Sofia .... "Wisdom" (*Greek*). Sophia was a favorite royal name with many German and Danish princesses. It came into popularity after the Roman Emperor Justinian built a church in Constantinople intended to outshine Solomon's temple and called it Sta. Sophia or "divine wisdom." DIM. Sophie, Sophy.

Sophronia .... "Of wise, or prudent, mind" (*Greek*).

Stacia, Stacie, Stacy .... "One who shall rise again" (*Greek*). Contractions of Anastasia.

Star .... "A star."

Stella .... "A star" (*Latin*).

Stephana, Stephania, Stefania .... "A crown or garland" (*Greek*). Feminine forms of Stephen.

Stephanie, Stefanie .... French forms of Stephana, above.

Sue .... "A lily" (*Hebrew*). A diminutive of Susan or Susannah.

Susan .... "A lily" (*Hebrew*). Properly a diminutive of Susannah, below, but used as an independent name.

Susannah, Susanna, Suzanna .... "A lily" (*Hebrew*). A Biblical name, perhaps originally from the city of Susa in Persia—so called because of the white lilies that grew there. DIM. Susan, Susie, Susy, Suky, Sue.

Susanne, Suzanne .... "A lily" (*Hebrew*). French forms of Susannah.

Susie, Susy .... "A lily" (*Hebrew*). Diminutives of Susan or Susannah.

Suzette .... "A lily" (*Hebrew*). A French diminutive of Susannah.

Swanhilda .... "Swan maiden" or "swan battle-maid" (*Teutonic*). Derived from the name of one of the Valkyrs, maidens who, in Norse mythology, bore the souls of slain warriors to paradise. Valkyrs were able to change themselves into swans.

Sylvana .... "Forest maiden" (*Latin*). Feminine of Silvanus.

Sylvia, Silvia .... "Forest maiden" (*Latin*). Feminines of Silvanus.

T

Tabitha .... "The gazelle" (*Aramaic*). The gazelle was anciently regarded as a standard of graceful beauty, and in Hebrew its name signifies "beauty." The Tabitha of the New Testament was a woman noted for her good works (Acts ix:36).

Talitha, Taletha .... "Damsel" (*Aramaic*).

Tallula .... In modern American usage a "place" name.

Tamara .... "The palm tree" (*Hebrew*). In Oriental countries the palm was used as a symbolic name because of the beauty and fruitfulness of the tree.

Tara .... The ancient Irish kings resided in "Tara's Halls," where the bards sang of the deeds of heroes. The ruins still stand on the hill of Tara, which means "crag" or "tower" (*Gaelic*).

Templa .... "A temple or sanctuary" (*Latin*).

Teresa, Terese .... "The harvester" (*Greek*).

Teresina, Teresita .... "The harvester" (*Greek*). Italian and Spanish diminutive forms of Theresa.

Tertia .... "The third" (*Latin*). A name sometimes given to a third child, if a girl.

Terza .... Either "the third" (*Italian*), or a form of Theresa, "the harvester" (*Greek*).

Tess .... "The harvester" (*Greek*). A diminutive of Theresa, but also used as an independent name.

Tessa .... Either "the fourth" (*Greek*), or a diminutive of Theresa, "the harvester" (*Greek*).

Thadine .... "The praised" (*Hebrew*). A feminine diminutive of Thaddeus.

Thaïs .... "The bond" (*Greek*). A name made famous by the mistress of Alexander the Great. Revived by Anatole France in his novel "Thaïs" (1890), upon which Massenet based his opera of the same title.

Thalia .... "Joyful, blooming" (*Greek*). In Greek mythology Thalia was one of the Three Graces and the Muse of Joy and Comedy.

Thea .... "Divine" (*Greek*). Thea, in Greek mythology, was one of the Titans, supernatural beings who opposed the Olympian gods.

Thecla, Thekla .... "Of divine fame" (*Greek*). A name commemorating St. Thecla, the first virgin martyr.

Theda .... Contracted from Theodora, below.

Thelma .... "Nursling" (*Greek*).

Theodora .... "Divine gift" (*Greek*). The feminine of Theodore.

Theodosia .... "Divine gift" (*Greek*). A feminine, through Theodosius, of Theodore.

Theola .... "The divine" (*Greek*).

Thera .... "The unmastered, or wild" (*Greek*).

Theresa, Therese .... "The harvester, or reaper" (*Greek*). DIM. Tess, Tessa, Terry.

Thetis .... In Greek mythology Thetis was a sea-nymph, the mother of Achilles. She dipped him when an infant into the river Styx to render him invulnerable, but forgot to immerse the heel by which she held him.

Thirza "Delight, pleasantness" (*Hebrew*).

Thisbe .... In Greek legend Thisbe was a maiden whose lover, Pyramus, killed himself when he believed she had been slain by a lion. The tale is burlesqued in Shakespeare's "Midsummer Night's Dream."

Thomasine, Thomasina .... "The twin" (*Hebrew*). Feminines of Thomas, which see.

Thora .... "Thunder" (*Teutonic*). From Thor, the god of Scandinavian mythology, friend of mankind and slayer of evil spirits. His name means "thunder."

Tilda .... This name, which taken by itself means "maid of battles" (*Teutonic*), is nowadays generally used as a contraction for Matilda.

Tilly, Tillie .... Diminutives of Matilda, which see.

Timothea .... "Honoring God" (*Greek*). Feminine of Timothy.

Tina .... A nickname for several female names ending in "tina," such as Christina, Martina, Bettina, etc.

Toinette .... "Beyond praise" (*Latin*). A contraction of Antoinette.

Tonia .... "Beyond praise" (*Latin*). A feminine diminutive of Antony.

Trella .... A short form of Estrella, the Spanish for Esther, meaning "a star."

Tressa .... "The harvester" (*Greek*). A short form of Theresa.

Trilby .... A name coined by George Du Maurier for the heroine of his popular novel of that title. Possibly suggested by Trili, a Swiss diminutive of Catherine.

Trina .... "Pure" (*Greek*). A diminutive of Catherine.

Trinette .... "Little Catherine." A "pet" diminutive of Catherine.

Trista .... "The sorrowful" (*Latin*). An independent name, but also the feminine of Tristan.

Trixy, Trix .... "She who blesses" (*Latin*). Diminutives of Beatrix.

Trude, Truda .... Abbreviations of Gertrude, "spearmaiden," in which name the "ger" means "spear" and the "trude," "maiden."

Trudel .... A Dutch contraction of Gertrude. See Trude, above.

U

Udele .... "Rich or prosperous" (*Anglo-Saxon*).

Ula .... "Jewel of the sea" (*Celtic*). Originally a diminutive of Cordula, a Welsh form of Cordelia.

Ulrica, Ulrika .... "Ruler of all" (*Teutonic*). Feminine forms of Ulric.

Una .... "The one" (*Latin*). In modern usage this name comes from Spenser's heroine in his "Faerie Queene" (1590), where she personifies truth, because all truth is one. But as an old Celtic name Una means "famine."

Undine .... "Of the waves" (*Latin*). Undine was a fabled water-nymph who gained a soul by marriage with a mortal.

Urania .... "The heavenly" (*Greek*). In Greek mythology Urania was the Muse of Astronomy.

Ursa .... In Greek mythology Ursa was a nymph transformed by Artemis into a bear, but later placed in heaven as a constellation (Ursa Major) by her lover Zeus. The name literally means "she-bear" (*Latin*).

Ursel .... A form of Ursula or Ursa. See Ursa.

Ursula .... The most popular form of Ursa, which see.

V

Val .... A feminine diminutive of Valentine, which means "the valorous, or strong" (*Latin*).

Valda .... "Spirited in battle" (*Teutonic*). Feminine of Valdis.

Valeda .... "The strong or healthy" (*Latin*).

Valencia, Valentia .... "The strong or vigorous" (*Latin*).

Valentina .... "The strong or valiant" (*Latin*). Feminine of Valentine.

Valerie .... "The strong or valorous" (*Latin*).

WHAT SHALL WE NAME THE BABY?

Valonia, Vallonia .... "Of the vale or valley" (*Latin*). Vallonia was the Latin goddess of valleys.

Valora .... "The valorous or brave" (*Latin*).

Vanessa .... "Butterfly" (*Greek*). Originally "Phanessa," who was the mystic goddess of an ancient Greek brotherhood.

Vania .... "God's gracious gift" (*Hebrew*). A feminine of Ivan, the Russian form of John.

Vara .... "The stranger" (*Greek*). A Slavonic diminutive of Barbara.

Vashti .... "Beautiful" (*Persian*). A Biblical character in the Book of Esther.

Veda .... "Knowledge, understanding" (*Sanskrit*).

Vedette .... "Watch tower" (*Old French*).

Vedis .... "Sacred spirit of the forest" (*Teutonic*).

Velda .... A shorter form of Veleda, below.

Veleda .... "Of inspired wisdom" (*Teutonic*). Veleda was an ancient Germanic prophetess of the first century A.D., regarded as divine.

Vera .... "The true" (*Latin*).

Veradis .... "Truthful, genuine" (*Latin*).

Verda .... "Spring-like, or fresh" (*Latin*).

Verna .... "Spring-born or vernal" (*Latin*).

Vernita .... A diminutive of Verna, above.

Veronica .... "True image" (*Latin-Greek*). It is related that on the way to Calvary a maiden handed Christ her handkerchief upon which His likeness thereafter miraculously appeared, whence she received her name.

Vesta .... In Roman mythology Vesta was the goddess of the hearth and home, and guardian of the sacred fire tended by the Vestal Virgins.

Victoria .... "The victorious" (*Latin*). Feminine of Victor.

Victorine .... "The victorious" (*Latin*). A French form of Victoria.

Vida .... "The beloved" (*Hebrew*). A contraction of Davida, the Welsh feminine for David. Also a Hungarian form of Vita, below.

Vidette .... "The beloved" (*Hebrew*). A feminine diminutive of David.

Vine .... A name from the clinging plant.

Viola .... An Italian form of Violet, below. Shakespeare chose this name for his heroine in "Twelfth Night."

Violet .... A "flower" name (*Old French-Latin*). The violet is symbolic of modesty from the shy habit of the woodland plant.

Violetta, Violette .... "Little violet"—the "etta" and "ette" endings mean "little."

Virginia .... "Virgin, maidenly, pure" (*Latin*). The state of Virginia was named by Sir Walter Raleigh in honor of Elizabeth "the virgin queen."

Viridis .... "Youthful and blooming" (*Latin*).

Vita .... "The vital or animated" (*Latin*).

Vivian .... "Animated, lively" (*Latin*). In the King Arthur legends Vivian was an enchantress who by her spells imprisoned Merlin.

117

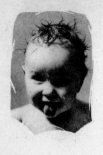 

Vivienne .... "Animated, lively" (*Latin*). A French form of Vivian.

Voleta, Voletta .... Perhaps "the veiled" (*Old French*), from "volet," a veil worn by women in the Middle Ages.

W

Wanda .... "The wanderer" (*Teutonic*).

Wandis .... A name of modern coinage. It may perhaps either be translated as "lithe and slender" from the Teutonic word for wand, or, like Wanda, mean "the wanderer."

Welcome .... A favorite Puritan name which carries its own meaning.

Wenda .... "The wanderer" (*Teutonic*).

Wendelin, Wendeline .... "The wender, or wanderer" (*Teutonic*).

Wenona, Wenonah .... "First-born daughter" (*American Indian*).

"Fair Nokomis bore a daughter,
  And she called her name Wenonah,
  As the first-born of her daughters."
                    —Longfellow's "Hiawatha."

Wesla .... Feminine of Wesley or Westley, an Old English "residence" name which means "from the west meadow."

Wilda .... Either "forest-dweller," or "the wayward or untamed" (*Anglo-Saxon*).

Wileen .... A contraction of Wilhelmina, below.

Wilhelmina .... "Resolute protectress" (*Teutonic*). The feminine of William. DIM. Mina, Minna, Mimi.

Willa .... "The desired" (*Anglo-Saxon*). Also a contraction of Wilhelmina, above.

Willabel, Willabelle .... Probably a modern combination of William and Belle.

Willette .... A feminine diminutive of William, which means "resolute protector" (*Teutonic*).

Wilmet .... A diminutive form of Wilhelmina, above.

Wilona, Wilone .... "The desired or wished-for" (*Anglo-Saxon*).

Winema .... "Chieftainess" (*American Indian*).

Winifred .... "Friend of peace" (*Teutonic*). DIM. Winnie.

Wynne .... "White, or fair" (*Celtic*).

X

Xanthe .... "The yellow-haired" (*Greek*).

Xenia .... "The hospitable" (*Greek*). Also spelled Zenia.

Xylia .... "Of the wood" (*Greek*).

Xylina .... "Of the wood" (*Greek*).

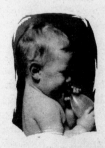

Y

Yolanda, Yolande .... A French historical name of
doubtful derivation. It may be a corrupt Latin
form of Valentina and mean "strong," or an elab-
oration of Viola, meaning "the violet."

Yolanthe .... A form of Yolanda, above.

Ysabel .... A Spanish form of Isabel, which see.

Yseult .... "The fair" (*Celtic*). An Old French spelling
of Isolde.

Yvette .... Another form of Yvonne, below.

Yvonne .... A popular French name, commemorating
the famous St. Yves, or Ivo, of Brittany. His name
sprang from the Scandinavian Iver, meaning
"archer."

Z

Zabrina .... Another spelling of Sabrina, which see.

Zamora .... A Spanish "place" name, from the ancient
historical province in Spain.

Zandra .... "Helper of mankind" (*Greek*). Another
spelling of Sandra, a feminine diminutive of Alexander.

Zaneta .... "God's gracious gift" (*Hebrew*). A Russian
feminine form of John.

Zara, Zarah .... Either "coming of light, or dawn" (*Hebrew*); or varied spellings of Sarah which means "the princess."

Zelda .... Short for Griselda, which see.

Zenda .... Probably from the Persian word "zendna" meaning "womanly."

Zenia .... "The hospitable" (*Greek*). Another spelling of Xenia.

Zenobia .... "Zeus-born" (*Greek*), or "her father's ornament" (*Arabic*). Zenobia was a famous conquering queen of Palmyra in the third century A.D.

Zerelda .... A name of doubtful derivation. Possibly based on Serilda, which means "armored warrior-maid" (*Teutonic*).

Zerlina .... A name probably coined for the rustic beauty in Mozart's opera "Don Giovanni" (1787).

Zita .... Perhaps short for Theresita, which means "the harvester" (*Greek*). St. Zita is the patron saint of Lucca, Italy.

Zoe .... "Life" (*Greek*). A Greek translation of the Hebrew "Eve."

Zora, Zorah .... "Dawn." Slavonic forms of Aurora. Aurora was the Latin goddess of dawn.

Zorana .... "Dawn." An elaborated form of Zora, above.

Boys' Names

Boys' Names

A

Aaron .... First high priest of the Jewish nation. The meaning of the name is obscure; probably either "the enlightened" or "mountain high" (*Hebrew*).

Abbot, Abbott .... "Father" (*Hebrew*); hence the father, or head, of a monastery.

Abbotson .... "Son of Abbot."

Abel .... "Breath" or "evanescence" (*Hebrew*). Adam's second son; perhaps prophetically so called from the shortness of his life.

Abelard .... "Nobly resolute" (*Teutonic*).

Abijah, Abisha .... "The Lord is my father" (*Hebrew*).

Abner .... "Father of light" (*Hebrew*).

Abraham .... "Father of multitudes" (*Hebrew*). The founder of the Hebrew race.

Abram .... "Exalted father" (*Hebrew*). The original name of Abraham.

Absalom .... "Father of peace" (*Hebrew*).

Achilles .... The mythical hero of Homer's "Iliad."

Ackerley, Ackley .... "From the oak tree meadow" (*Old English*). A "residence" name.

Adair .... "From the ford by the oak trees." A Celtic "residence" name.

Adal .... "Noble" (*Teutonic*).

Adalard, Adelard .... "Nobly brave" (*Teutonic*).

Adam "Man of red earth" (*Hebrew*). So called be-

125

cause the soil of Palestine from which he, the first man, was created is red. The name has come to signify "human" or "mortal."

Adams .... Short for "Adam's son."

Adamson .... "Son of Adam."

Addis .... "Son of Addy." Addy was an Old English contraction of Adam.

Addison .... "Son of Addis"; but as Addis means "son of Adam," Addison literally means "descendant of Adam."

Adelbert, Adalbert .... "Nobly bright" (*Teutonic*). A German form of Albert.

Adelric, Adalric .... "Noble commander" (*Teutonic*).

Adin .... "Delicate" (*Hebrew*).

Adlar .... "Noble and brave" (*Teutonic*).

Adley .... "The just" (*Hebrew*).

Adolphus, Adolph, Adolf .... "Noble wolf" (*Teutonic*). The wolf was highly respected in olden times; see Foreword.

Adon .... "Lord" (*Hebrew*).

Adonis .... A Greek form of Adon. The Adonis of classic mythology was a beautiful youth beloved by Venus, whence the name came to signify "handsome."

Adrian, Adrien .... "From Adria, Italy," whence the Adriatic Sea (*Latin*). As Hadrian the name was borne by a Roman emperor and six Popes.

Adriel .... "Of God's flock" (*Hebrew*).

Æneas .... "Praiseworthy" (*Greek*). The ancestral hero of the Roman nation and of Vergil's "Æneid."

Ahern, Ahearn .... "Lord of the horses" (*Celtic*).

Aidan .... "Fire" (*Celtic*); but linked with the Latin word for "hearth," and so signifying "warmth of the home."

Aiken .... "The oaken," signifying sturdiness (*Anglo-Saxon*).

Ainsley, Ainslie .... "From Ann's meadow." An Old English "residence" name. But Ann, in Anglo-Saxon, was a male personal name.

Ainsworth .... "From Ann's estate." An Old English "residence" name. Compare Ainsley.

Airell .... Probably a Celtic variant of Earl, meaning "nobleman" or "chief."

Ajax .... "Eagle" (*Greek*). A legendary hero in Homer's "Iliad," distinguished for strength and bravery.

Alair .... Possibly derived from Hilary, meaning "cheerful" (*Latin*).

Alan, Allan, Allen .... "Comely or fair" (*Celtic*).

Alanson .... "Son of Alan," see above.

Alaric, Alrick, Alric .... "Ruler of all" (*Teutonic*). The Gothic king who conquered Rome.

Alban, Albin .... "White or fair" (*Latin*). See Albion.

Albern .... "Of noble valor," literally "noble bear" (*Teutonic*). The bear was synonymous with courage.

Albert .... "Noble and brilliant" (*Teutonic*). This name, originally Adelbrecht, was spread in various forms throughout Europe by a missionary and saint who was a brother of the English King Alfred. Its popularity in England was revived by the Prince Consort, husband of Queen Victoria.

Albion .... "White or fair" (*Latin*). Albion, or "the white cliffs," was the ancient name for Britain, including Scotland.

Alcott .... "From the old cottage" (*Old English*). A "residence" name.

Alden, Aldin .... "Old friend or protector" (*Anglo-Saxon*).

Aldis, Aldus, Aldous .... "From the old house" (*Old English*). A "residence" name.

 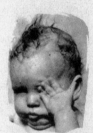

Aldo "Rich" (*Italian-Teutonic*).

Aldred .... "Ancient counselor" (*Anglo-Saxon*).

Aldrich, Aldric .... "Sage, or noble, ruler" (*Teutonic*).

Aldridge .... A form of Aldrich, above.

Aldwin .... "Old friend or protector" (*Anglo-Saxon*).

Aleron .... An "aileron" (*Old French*), from which the name is derived, was a shoulder-badge, or epaulet, worn by a knight. So Aleron signifies "knight."

Alexander .... "Helper of mankind" (*Greek*). A name made famous by the conqueror Alexander the Great. DIM. Alex, Sandy.

Alford, Alvord .... Either "from the old ford," an Old English "residence" name, or derived from Alfred.

Alfred .... "Supernaturally wise" (*Teutonic*); literally "of elf-counsel." Elves were anciently esteemed as supernatural beings who influenced, and sometimes advised, mortals. The English King Alfred the Great conquered the Danes and originated the English Navy.

Alger, Algar .... "Noble, or experienced, spearman" (*Anglo-Saon*).

Algernon .... "Bearded" (*Old French*).

Alison, Allison .... "Of holy fame" (*Teutonic*).

Allard, Alard .... "Nobly resolute" (*Teutonic*).

Allister, Alaster .... Gaelic variants of Alexander, above.

Almund .... Either "protector of the temple" (*Anglo-Saxon*), or "the German" (*Teutonic*).

Alonzo .... A form of Alphonso, below.

Aloysius .... "Famous in war" (*Teutonic*).

Alpheus .... Either "river god," from the mythical Greek hunter who was changed into a river; or if from the Hebrew "one exchanged or substituted."

Alphonso, Alfonso .... "Eager for battle" (*Teutonic*). A frequent royal name in Spanish history.

Alroy .... "Royal" (*Latin*).

Alson .... "Son of All." "All" was an Old English form of Alan.

Alston .... "From the elf's abode" (*Old English*).

Alton .... "From the old manor or village" (*Old English*). A "residence" name.

Alvar, Alver .... "White or fair" (*Latin*).

Alvin, Alvan .... "Beloved by all" (*Teutonic*).

Alvis .... In Norse mythology the suitor for the god Thor's daughter.

Alwin, Alwyn .... Forms of Alvin, above.

Amadis .... "Love of God" (*Latin*).

Amasa .... "Burden" (*Hebrew*).

Ambert .... "Bright" (*Teutonic*).

Ambrose "Immortal" (*Greek*).

Amery, Amory "Industrious" (*Teutonic*). America was so called from the discoverer Amerigo Vespucci, who bore the name Amery in its Italian form. Amory may also be from the Latin, "loveable."

Amiel .... "Of the Lord's people" (*Hebrew*).

Amos .... "A burden" (*Hebrew*).

Amsden .... An Old English "residence" name signifying "from the valley owned by Ambrose."

Amyas, Amias "One who shall love God" (*Latin*).

Anastasius .... "One who shall rise again" (*Greek*).

Anatol .... "From the east" (*Greek*). A name sometimes given to a child born at sunrise.

Anders .... A Danish form of Andrew, below.

Anderson .... "Son of Andrew."

Andrew .... "Manly" (*Greek*). One of the twelve disciples. St. Andrew is the patron saint of Scotland, Prussia and Russia.

Angell .... "Messenger" (*Greek*).

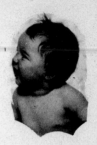

Angus .... "Exceptionally strong" (*Celtic*).

Anselm, Ansel .... "Divine helmet" (*Teutonic*); but, as the ancient helmet signified protection, the name may be rendered "divine protector."

Anson .... "Son of Ann"; but Ann was once an Anglo-Saxon masculine name, although contracted from Hannah.

Anstice .... A contraction of Anastasius, above.

Anthony, Antony .... "Inestimable, or beyond praise" (*Latin*). St. Anthony is the patron saint of Italy. DIM. Tony.

Apollo .... The Greek god of light, healing, and the arts. His name symbolizes "manly beauty."

Arber .... "Dealer in herbs" (*Old French-Latin*).

Archer .... "Bowman" (*Latin*).

Archibald .... "Sacred and bold" or "sacred prince" (*Teutonic*). DIM. Archy, Archie.

Ardel, Ardell .... "From the hares' dell or valley." An Old English "residence" name.

Arden, Ardin .... "Fervent or eager" (*Latin*).

Arend .... An Old Dutch form of Arnold, below.

Argus .... "All-seeing" or "vigilant." From Argus, a giant of Greek mythology who had a hundred eyes.

Argyle .... "From the land of the Irish" (*Celtic*). The Scotch county of this name was originally settled by an Irish king.

WHAT SHALL WE NAME THE BABY?

Aric, Arick .... "Ruler" (*Teutonic*).

Arkwright .... "Maker of chests" (*Old English*). An "occupation" name.

Arlen, Arlin .... "A pledge" (*Celtic*).

Arley, Arlie .... From the Old English "residence" name Harley, which means "the hare meadow."

Arlo .... Probably a contraction of the Old English "residence" name Harlow, or "fortified hill."

Armand .... A French variant of Armin, below. St. Armand is the patron saint of the Netherlands.

Armin .... The original meaning of this name is obscure. It is, however, sometimes traced to Herman, which signifies "war man, or warrior" (*Teutonic*).

Armstrong .... "Strong of arm." An Old English nickname, which later became a surname.

Arnold .... "Mighty as the eagle" (*Teutonic*).

Artemas, Artemus .... "Gift of the goddess Artemis" (*Greek*). The Greek Artemis was goddess of the chase and of the moon, like the Roman Diana.

Arthur .... A favorite name of puzzling origin. It may be safely interpreted as "valorous," since its Welsh form, "bear-man," suggests bravery, and an Old Celtic derivation, "rock," suggests firmness. Its English popularity springs from King Arthur, mythical hero of the Round Table legends.

Arundel .... "From the eagle dell" (*Old English*). A "residence" name.

Arvel .... "Wept over" (*Welsh*). Probably first used as a surname to commemorate some esteemed ancestor—like our "late lamented."

Arvin .... "Friend of the people" (*Teutonic*).

Asa .... "Healer or physician" (*Hebrew*).

Ashby .... "From the ash tree farm" (*Scandinavian*). A "residence" name.

Asher .... "Happy or fortunate" (*Hebrew*).

Ashford .... "Dweller by the ash tree ford" (*Old English*).

Ashley .... "Dweller in the ash tree meadow" (*Old English*).

Ashton .... "From the ash tree farm" (*Old English*). A "residence" name.

Athmore .... "From the moor." An Old English "residence" name.

Atwater .... "From the water-side" (*Old English*). A "residence" name.

Atwell .... "Dweller by the spring" (*Old English*).

Atwood .... "Forest dweller" (*Old English*). A "residence" name.

Aubin, Aubyn .... "White or fair" (*Latin*). Compare Albion.

Aubrey .... "Ruler of the elves" (*Teutonic*). Elves were formerly believed to influence mortals, for good or ill.

Audley .... An Anglo-Saxon name of obscure meaning.

Audwin .... "Rich or prospering friend" (*Teutonic*).

August, Augustin .... Variants of Augustus, below.

Augustus .... "The exalted, sacred, or sublime" (*Latin*). A title conferred upon the first Roman emperor, Augustus Caesar.

Aurick .... Possibly another spelling of Warrick, which see.

Austin .... A shortened form of Augustus, above.

Averil, Averill .... Either from "averil," the Anglo Saxon name for the month of April; or, if from the Old English, signifying "wild boar."

Avery .... "Ruler of the elves" (*Anglo-Saxon*). Elve were formerly revered as powerful, supernatura beings.

Axel, Aksel .... "Father of peace" (*Hebrew*). Forms o Absalom. The first is a national Danish name.

Aylmer, Aylmar .... "Of awe-inspiring fame" (*Teu tonic*).

Aylsworth .... "Of awe-inspiring worth" (*Teutonic*).

Aylward .... "Formidable guardian" (*Teutonic*).

Aylwin .... "Awe-inspiring friend" (*Teutonic*).

B

Bailey, Bayley .... "Bailiff or steward" (*Old French*) An "occupation" name.

Bainbridge .... "Dweller by the bridge over the clea stream" (*Gaelic*). A "residence" name.

Baird .... "Bard or minstrel" (*Celtic*). An "occupation" name.

Baldwin .... "Bold or princely friend" (*Teutonic*).

Balfour .... This Scotch name may come from the Gaelic word for "pasture-land."

Bancroft .... "From the bean field" (*Old English*). A "residence" name.

Barden .... "Dweller near the boars' den" (*Old English*).

Bardo .... A Danish form of Bartholomew, below.

Barlow .... Either "dweller on the bare hill" or "on the boars' hill." An Old English "residence" name.

Barnabas .... "Son of prophecy" (*Hebrew*).

Barnaby .... A form of Barnabas, above.

Barrett .... "Bear-like" (*Teutonic*).

Barron .... "Noble warrior" (*Teutonic*). The English barons originally gained the title by military service.

Barry .... "Dweller at the barrier or rampart" (*Old French*).

Bartholomew .... "Son of the furrows," therefore "ploughman" (*Hebrew*). DIM. Bart.

Bartlett .... Probably an Old French form of Bartholomew, above.

Bartley .... A short form of Bartholomew, above.

Barton .... "From the barley farm." An Old English "residence" name.

Basil .... "Kingly" (*Greek*).

Baxter .... "Baker" (*Old English*). A "trade" name.

Bayard .... "With red-brown hair" (*Teutonic*).

Beaufort .... "From the fine fortress." An Old French "residence" name.

Bela .... "Destruction (*Hebrew*). A Biblical name taken from the city destroyed by earthquakes.

Belden .... "From the fair valley" (*Teutonic*). A "residence" name.

Benedict .... "Blessed" (*Latin*). A name assumed by fifteen Popes. As a modern byword for a confirmed bachelor who marries, it dates from Shakespeare's hero in "Much Ado About Nothing."

Benjamin .... "Son of the right hand," signifying "fortunate" (*Hebrew*). Founder of the Hebrew tribe bearing his name.

Bennett .... A short form of Benedict, above.

WHAT SHALL WE NAME THE BABY?

Benton .... "Moor dweller" (*Old English*). A "residence" name.

Berkeley, Barclay .... "From the birch meadow." An Anglo-Saxon "residence" name.

Bernard, Barnard .... "Brave, or bear-strong, warrior" (*Teutonic*). DIM. Barney.

Bert .... "Bright" (*Teutonic*). An individual name; also a short form of Bertram, and of several names ending in "bert," like Albert, etc.

Berton .... "Glorious raven" (*Teutonic*). A variant of Bertram.

Bertram, Bartram, Bertrand .... "Bright or glorious raven" (*Teutonic*). The raven was a bird anciently esteemed. See Foreword.

Bertwin .... "Bright or shining friend" (*Teutonic*).

Berwick .... "From the barley grange." An Old English "residence" name.

Berwin .... "Warrior friend" (*Teutonic*).

Bevan, Bevin .... "Son of Evan." Evan means "youthful warrior" (*Celtic*).

Beverley .... "From the beaver meadow." An Old English "residence" name.

Bevis .... Either "bowman" (*Teutonic*), or "from the French city of Beauvais."

Blagdon, Blagden .... "From the dark valley." An Old English "residence" name.

Blaine, Blainey, Blayney .... Celtic nicknames meaning "the thin or lean."

Blair .... "From the plain" (*Celtic*). A "residence" name.

Blake .... Either "black" or "pallid," according to the Old English root-word chosen—a case where black may be white!

Blandon .... "Gentle" (*Latin*).

Bliss .... "Happy" (*Anglo-Saxon*).

Bolton .... "Of the manor farm." An Old English "residence" name.

Booth .... "From the market-stall or booth" (*Teutonic*). A "residence" name.

Borden .... "From the boar valley." An Anglo-Saxon "residence" name.

Boris .... "Warrior" (*Slavonic*).

Bowden, Boden .... Forms of Boyden, below.

Bowen .... Originally Ap-Owen, or "son of Owen" (*Celtic*). See Owen.

Boyce .... "Woodland dweller" (*Teutonic*). Compare the French "bois."

Boyd .... "Yellow-haired" (*Celtic*).

Boyden .... Either "a herald" (*Anglo-Saxon*), or "yellow-haired" (*Celtic*).

Boynton .... "From the Irish river Boyne" or "white cow river" (*Celtic*).

Braden .... "From the broad valley" (*Old English*). A "residence" name.

Bradford .... "From the broad ford." An Old English "residence" name.

Bradley .... "From the broad meadow" (*Old English*). A "residence" name.

Bradwell .... "From the broad, or wide, spring." An Old English "residence" name.

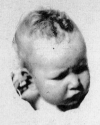

Brainard .... "Bold raven" (*Teutonic*). For the significance of the raven see Foreword.

Brandon .... "One from the lighted, or beacon, hill" (*Teutonic*). A "residence" name.

Brant .... "Firebrand" (*Teutonic*).

Brent .... "From the steep hill." An Old English "residence" name.

Brett .... "A Breton" or native of Brittany (*Celtic*).

Brian, Bryan .... "The strong" (*Celtic*).

Brice, Bryce .... "Quick moving" (*Celtic*).

Brigham .... "Dweller by the bridge" (*Old English*).

Brinton .... A "place" name from the English town of Brinton in Norfolk.

Brock .... An Old English nickname meaning "the badger."

Broderick .... From the Welsh Ap-Roderick, or "son of Roderick."

Bromley .... "From the broom-covered meadow." An Old English "residence" name.

Bronson .... "Son of Brun—the dark-skinned." "Brun" was the Anglo-Saxon form of Brown.

Brooks .... "Dweller by the stream" (*Old English*). A "residence" name.

Bruce .... A "place" name from the town of Bruys, in Normandy. Bruys means "the brushwood thicket" (*Old French*).

Bruno .... "Of brown, or dark, complexion" (*Teutonic*).

Bryant .... "Strong" (*Celtic*).

138

Burgess .... A citizen of a town, or a burgess (*Teutonic*).

Burke .... "Stronghold or castle" (*Teutonic*).

Burleigh, Burley .... A Teutonic "residence" name, probably meaning "from the meadow by the hill or castle."

Byram .... "Of the cattle-yard, or byre" (*Old English*). A "residence" name.

Byron .... "From the cottage" (*Teutonic*). A name made famous by Lord Byron, the English poet.

C

Cadell .... "Of martial spirit" (*Celtic*).

Cadman .... "Warrior" (*Celtic*).

Cadmar .... "Mighty in battle" (*Celtic*).

Caesar .... Probably "long-haired" (*Latin*). The title Caesar, from the name of Julius Caesar, the Roman general and dictator, was assumed by succeeding Roman emperors; and with the significance of "imperial" became "Kaiser" in German and "Tsar" in Russian.

Calder .... "From the stony river" (*Celtic*). A "residence" name.

Caleb .... Meaning "dog" (*Hebrew*), with the significance of faithful affection.

Calvert, Calbert .... "Herdsman" (*Old English*). An "occupation" name.

Calvin .... "Bald" (*Latin*). A name made famous by the Protestant reformer John Calvin.

139

Cameron .... "Crooked nose" (*Celtic*). Probably originally the nickname of some Highland chieftain so afflicted.

Campbell .... "From the fair field" (*Old French*). A "residence" name.

Cardew .... "From the black fort." A Celtic "residence" name.

Carew .... "From the fortress" (*Celtic*). A "residence" name.

Carey, Cary .... Same meaning as Carew, above.

Carl, Carlo .... Variants of Charles, which see.

Carleton, Carlton .... "From Carl's farm" (*Old English*). A "residence" name.

Carlisle, Carlyle .... "From the walled city" (*Old English-Latin*). A "residence" name.

Carney .... "Warrior" (*Celtic*).

Carroll, Carrol .... "Champion" (*Celtic*).

Carson .... "Son of Carr." "Carr" is a Scandinavian proper name meaning "dweller by the marsh."

Carter .... "Cart-driver." An Old English "occupation" name.

Carvel, Carvell .... "From the villa by the marsh" (*Old English*). A "residence" name.

Carver .... "Wood-carver or sculptor." An Old English "occupation" name.

Casey .... "Valorous" (*Celtic*).

Caspar .... A form of Gaspar, the name of one of the Three Wise Men led by the star to Bethlehem. Probably from the Persian word for "treasure."

Cass .... Probably from the Latin name Cassius, meaning "vain."

Caton .... From the Latin name Cato, meaning "sagacious."

Cavell .... "Boldly active" (*Teutonic*).

Cecil .... "Blind" (*Latin*).

Cedric .... "Chieftain" (*Celtic*).

Chadburn .... "From the wildcat brook." An Old English "residence" name.

Chadwick .... "From the warrior's town" (*Old English-Celtic*). A "residence" name.

Chalmer, Chalmers .... "Lord of the household, or chamberlain" (*Teutonic*).

Chandler, Chanler .... "Candle-maker." An Old French "trade" name.

Channing .... "A canon," or member of a bishop's council. An Old French "occupation" name derived from the Latin.

Chapin .... "A chaplain, or clergyman" (*Old French*). Originally Chaplin.

Chapman .... "Merchant or trader" (*Anglo-Saxon*). An "occupation" name.

Chappell, Chappel .... "From the chapel." An Old French "residence" name.

Charles .... Literally the name means "man" (*Teutonic*); but, as borne by many kings and emperors, it took on a significance of greatness. Legend says that its most famous bearer, Charlemagne, was so called because when his nurse presented him to his mother she exclaimed, "What a great carle (man)!"

Charlton .... "From Charles' farm." An Old English "residence" name.

Chatwin .... "Warlike friend" (*Old English*).

Chauncey .... "Chancellor"—an official of church or state (*Latin*).

Cheney .... "From the oak-wood" (*Old French*). A "residence" name.

Chester, Cheston .... "Dweller in a fortified town" (*Old English*), from the Latin word for "camp."

Chilton .... "From the farm by the spring" (*Old English*). A "residence" name.

Christian .... "Follower of Christ." In Greek Christ signifies "the anointed."

Christie .... A Scotch form of Christian, above.

Christopher .... "Christ-bearer" (*Greek*). St. Christopher was so named because he is said to have borne the Christ-child across a river. He is the patron saint of travelers by land and sea. DIM. Chris, Kit.

Clarence .... "Illustrious" (*Latin*).

Claude .... "Lame" (*Latin*).

Clay .... "Man of clay, or mortal" (*Teutonic*).

Clayborne, Clayborn .... "Born of clay, or mortal" (*Teutonic*).

Clayton .... "From the town on the clay bed" (*Teutonic*). A "residence" name.

Clement, Clemence .... "Merciful" (*Latin*). DIM. Clem.

Clifford .... "Dweller at the ford near the cliff" (*Old English*).

Clifton .... "From the farm at the cliff" (*Old English*).

Clinton .... "From the headland farm" (*Teutonic*).

Clive .... "Cliff-dweller" (*Old English*).

Clyde .... "Heard from afar" (*Welsh*). The River Clyde was so named because of the roar of its falls.

Colby .... "From the black farm"—possibly a farm where coal was found. An Old English "residence" name.

Colin .... A diminutive of Nicholas, which means "people's victory" (*Greek*).

Collis .... "Son of the dark man." An Old English nickname.

Colman, Coleman .... "Dove" (*Irish*). More than one hundred Irish saints bear this name.

Colton .... "From the dark, or black, town" (*Old English*). A "residence" name.

Con, Conn .... "Wise" (*Celtic*). Sometimes used as short for Cornelius, though that name has a different source.

Conant, Conan .... "Wise" (*Celtic*).

Condon .... "The dark-haired Conn"—Conn meaning "wise" (*Celtic*).

Conrad .... "Able in counsel" (*Teutonic*).

Conroy .... "Wise man" (*Irish*).

Constantine .... "The constant, or firm of purpose" (*Latin*). Constantine, the first Christian Roman emperor, made the city of Byzantium his capital and changed its name to Constantinople.

Conway .... "Hound of the plain" (*Celtic*).

Corbin .... "The raven" (*Latin*). The raven was anciently the badge of a warrior. See Foreword.

Corey .... An Old Irish "residence" name, perhaps meaning "from the round hill."

Cornelius .... Of doubtful origin, but possibly from the Latin words for "war horn."

Corwin .... The same as Corbin, above.

143

 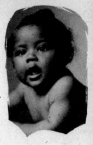

Cosmo .... From the Greek word for the universe, or cosmos, meaning "well-ordered." St. Cosmos is the patron saint of physicians and surgeons.

Courtland .... "From the enclosed land, or court" (*Anglo-French*). A "residence" name.

Courtney, Courtnay .... Forms of Courtland, above.

Craig .... "Crag-dweller" (*Scotch*).

Crandall, Crandell .... "From the valley of the cranes." An Old English "residence" name.

Crawford .... "From the crow ford," or ford where crows flock. An Old English "residence" name.

Creighton, Crichton .... "From the town, or farm, by the creek" (*Scotch-English*). A "residence" name.

Crispin .... "Curly-haired" (*Latin*).

Crofton .... "From the fenced, or enclosed, farm." An Old English "residence" name.

Crompton .... "From the winding, or crooked, farm" (*Old English*). A "residence" name.

Cromwell .... "Dweller by the winding brook." An Old English "residence" name made famous by Oliver Cromwell.

Crosby .... "Dweller by the town cross" (*Teutonic*).

Culbert, Colbert .... "Cool and brilliant" (*Teutonic*).

Cullen .... A Celtic pet name for a cub or young animal.

Culver .... "Dove" (*Old English*).

Curt .... "Short, or little" (*Latin*).

Curtis .... "Courteous, or court-bred" (*Old French*).

Cuthbert .... "Famous and brilliant" (*Anglo-Saxon*).

Cutler .... "Knife-maker." An Old English "trade" name.

Cuyler .... Of uncertain origin; possibly from the Irish "kyle" meaning "chapel."

Cyril .... "Lordly" (*Greek*).

Cyrus .... "The sun" (*Persian*). A name made famous by Cyrus the Great, founder of the Persian Empire.

D

Dale .... "Dweller in the dale" (*Teutonic*). A "residence" name.

Dallas .... "Dweller by the waterfall." A Celtic "residence" name.

Dalston .... An Anglo-Saxon name meaning "from Daegal's place"—Daegal being a Scandinavian personal name signifying "day, or dawn."

Dalton .... "From the farm in the dale" (*Old English*).

Damon .... From the Damon of ancient Syracuse who offered his life for his friend Pythias. The name has therefore come to suggest "loyal friendship."

Dana, Dane, Dain .... "A Dane, or one from Denmark" (*Scandinavian*).

Daniel .... "God is my judge" (*Hebrew*). Daniel was one of the great Biblical prophets. DIM. Dan.

Dannel .... A Teutonic form of Daniel, above.

Darcy .... Either "dark," from the Celtic; or, if from the Old French, "dweller in the stronghold."

Darnell, Darnall .... Either from the English town of Darnall, or a nickname from the darnel, a weed supposed to cause intoxication or madness.

Darrell, Daryl .... "Beloved or dear" (*Old English*).

Darrick .... Short for Theodoric, "ruler of the people" (*Teutonic*).

Darton .... "From the deer park" (*Old English*). A "residence" name.

David .... "Beloved one" (*Hebrew*). David was the second King of Israel. St. David is the patron saint of Wales. DIM. Dave, Davy, Davie.

Davin, Daven .... Literally "bright Finn"—or bright man from Finland (*Scandinavian*).

Davis An Old Scotch contraction of "David's son."

Dean, Deane .... "From the valley or dene." An Old English "residence" name.

Dearborn .... "Beloved child or bairn" (*Old English*).

Dedrick, Dedric .... Short for Theodoric, "ruler of the people" (*Teutonic*).

Delmer, Delmar .... "Mariner" (*Old French-Latin*).

Delwin .... "Valley friend," or friend from the valley (*Teutonic*).

Dempster .... "A judge" (*Old English*).

Denby .... "From the Danish settlement" (*Anglo-Scandinavian*). A "residence" name.

Denley .... "From the valley meadow." An Old English "residence" name.

Dennet .... A form of Dennis, below.

 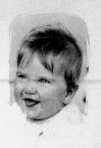

Dennis, Denis, Denys .... From Dionysos, the Greek god of wine. St. Denis is the patron saint of France.

Denton .... "From the valley farm." An Old English "residence" name.

Derrick .... Short for Theodoric, "ruler of the people" (*Teutonic*).

Derwin .... The meaning is uncertain, but perhaps may be interpreted as "friend of the wild deer, or wild animals" (*Old English-Teutonic*).

Desmond Either "gracious protector" (*Anglo-Saxon*); or, if from the Celtic, "man from South Munster"—the Irish province.

Devin .... "Poet" (*Celtic*).

Dexter .... "Dexterous or right-handed" (*Latin*).

Dickson, Dixon "Son of Dick" (*Old English*). Dick is a nickname for Richard, which means "powerful ruler" (*Teutonic*).

Dillon .... "Faithful and true" (*Celtic*).

Dinsmore .... "From the great hill fort." A Celtic "residence" name.

Dion .... Short for Dionysos, the Greek god of wine.

Dirk .... "Ruler of the people" (*Teutonic*).

Doane .... "From the sand hill or dune." A Celtic "residence" name.

Dominic, Dominick .... "The Lord's" (*Latin*). A name often given to a boy born on Sunday.

Don .... "Dark or brown" (*Celtic*), or "lord" (*Latin*). A name used independently, or as a contraction of Donald.

147

Donald .... Either "dark, or brown-haired, stranger" (*Celtic*); or, if through the Celtic-Latin, "lord."

Doran, Dorran .... "Stranger" (*Celtic*).

Dorian .... "A Dorian" (*Greek*). The Dorians were a famous people of ancient Greece, named from Dorus, the mythical founder. The sturdy simplicity of the race characterizes the Doric order of architecture.

Douglas .... "Dweller by the dark stream" (*Celtic*).

Doyle "Dark stranger" (*Celtic*).

Driscoll "Interpreter" (*Celtic*).

Druce A name of most uncertain origin. Possibly from the ancient "druid" or "wise man" (*Celtic*).

Dudley .. An Old English "residence" name from the town of Dudley, England.

Duer .... "Heroic" (*Celtic*).

Duke .. "Leader" (*Latin*).

Duncan .. "Dark-skinned warrior" (*Celtic*).

Dunstan "From the brown rock, or quarry." An Old English "residence" name.

Dunton .... "From the farmstead on the hill" (*Old English*). A "residence" name.

Durant, Durand .... "Enduring" (*Latin*).

Durward .... "Keeper of the gate or door" (*Old English*).

Durwin .... "Beloved friend" (*Anglo-Saxon*).

Dustin .... Possibly meaning "valiant" (*Teutonic*).

Dwight .... "White or fair" (*Teutonic*).

E

Earl, Earle .... "Nobleman or chief" (*Anglo-Saxon*).

Eaton .... "From the riverside village" (*Old English*). A "residence" name.

Eben .... "Rock" (*Hebrew*). Also a diminutive of Ebenezer.

Ebenezer .... "Rock of help" (*Hebrew*).

Edan .... "Fiery" (*Celtic*).

Edgar .... "Fortunate spear" (*Anglo-Saxon*), signifying what might correspond to our "happy warrior."

Edlin .... "Prosperous friend" (*Anglo-Saxon*). A form of Edwin.

Edmund, Edmond .... "Prosperous protector" (*Anglo-Saxon*).

Edric .... "Prosperous ruler" (*Anglo-Saxon*).

Edsel .... "From the hall owned by Ed." Ed was an Anglo-Saxon personal name meaning "prosperous."

Edson .... "Son of Ed." See Edward or Edwin.

Edward .... "Prosperous guardian" (*Anglo-Saxon*). Here the first syllable, "Ed," as in other Anglo-Saxon names, signifies prosperity in general, and may be translated as either "rich," "valuable," "fortunate," or "blessed." DIM. Ed, Ned, Ted, Teddy.

Edwin .... "Valuable friend" (*Anglo-Saxon*). For diminutives see Edward.

Egan, Egon .... Either "ardent" (*Celtic*), or "formidable" (*Teutonic*).

Egbert .... "Formidably brilliant" (*Teutonic*).

Egerton .... A "residence" name perhaps meaning "from the town on the ridge" (*Old English*).

Elbert .... "Nobly brilliant" (*Teutonic*).

Elden, Eldon .... Either "from the valley of the elves" (*Old English*), or "the elder" (*Teutonic*).

Eldred, Eldrid .... "Sage counselor" (*Anglo-Saxon*).

Eldwin .... "Sage friend" (*Anglo-Saxon*).

Eleazar, Eliezer .... "The Lord hath helped" (*Hebrew*)

Eli .... "The highest" (*Hebrew*).

Elias .... "Jehovah is God" (*Hebrew*).

Elihu .... "Jehovah is God" (*Hebrew*).

Elijah .... "Jehovah is God" (*Hebrew*). Elijah was a Hebrew prophet, called Elias in the New Testament.

Eliot, Eliott, Elliot .... French forms of Elias, above.

Elisha .... "God is salvation" (*Hebrew*).

Ellard .... "Nobly brave" (*Teutonic*).

Ellery, Ellary .... "Dweller by the alder tree" (*Teutonic*).

Ellis .... A form of Elias, above.

Ellison, Elson .... "Son of Elias."

Elmer, Elmar .... "Of awe-inspiring fame" (*Teutonic*)

Elroy .... "Royal" (*Latin*).

Elton .... "From the old farmstead." An Old English "residence" name.

Elwin, Elwyn, Elvin .... "Befriended by the elves" (*Anglo-Saxon*).

Ely .... Short for Elias, above.

Emerson .... "Son of Emery."

Emery, Emory .... "Industrious" (*Teutonic*). Compare Amelia.

Emil .... "Industrious" (*Teutonic*). Compare Amelia.

Emlen, Emelen, Emelin .... "Industrious" (*Teutonic*) Compare Amelia.

Emmanuel, Emanuel .... "God with us" (*Hebrew*).

Emmett, Emmet .... From the Anglo-Saxon nickname meaning "ant," and so suggesting diligence.

Enoch .... "Dedicated" (*Hebrew*).

Enos .... "Mortal" (*Hebrew*).

Ephraim, Ephrem .... "Doubly fruitful" (*Hebrew*).

Erasmus .... "Amiable" (*Greek*).

Erastus .... "Beloved" (*Greek*).

Eric, Erik, Erick .... "Ever powerful or kingly" (*Teutonic*).

Erland .... "Stranger or foreigner" (*Teutonic*).

Ernald .... "Noble eagle" (*Teutonic*).

Ernest .... "Intent in purpose" (*Teutonic*). Sometimes also traced to the Teutonic word for "eagle."

Errol .... Probably from Earl, "a nobleman" (*Teutonic*).

Erskine .... A "residence" name from the town of Erskine in Scotland. The meaning is unknown.

Erwin .... "Friend, or lover, of the sea" (*Anglo-Saxon*).

Esmond .... "Gracious protector" (*Anglo-Saxon*).

Ethan .... "The strong or firm" (*Hebrew*).

Ethelbert .... "Of shining nobility" (*Teutonic*).

Eugene .... "Well-born" (*Greek*). DIM. Gene.

Eustace, Eustis .... "Fruitful" (*Greek*).

Evan .... Either "well-born" (*Greek*), or "young warrior" (*Celtic*).

Evelyn .... Of no connection with the female Evelyn, but originally Avelin, an Old French male name from a Teutonic root meaning "ancestor."

Everard .... "Strong, or brave, as the wild boar" (*Teutonic*).

Everet, Everett .... Forms of Everard, above.

Evers .... "Wild boar" (*Anglo-Saxon*). The boar was in primitive days, a respected antagonist.

Ezekiel .... "Strength of the Lord" (*Hebrew*).

Ezra .... "The helper" (*Hebrew*).

F

Fabian .... "Bean farmer" (*Latin*). An "occupation" name.

Fabron .... "Mechanic" (*Latin*). A "trade" name, from the title of a famous ancient Roman clan, the Fabricii, or "mechanics"—so called from the nickname of some ancestor.

Fairfax .... "Fair-haired" (*Anglo-Saxon*).

Farley, Farleigh .... "From the bull pasture" (*Old English*). A "residence" name.

Farman .... "Traveler" (*Anglo-Saxon*).

Farrel, Farrell .... "Man of valor" (*Celtic*).

Faxon .... "Thick-haired" (*Teutonic*).

Felix .... "Fortunate" (*Latin*).

Fenris .... The name of a gigantic wolf in Norse mythology.

Fenton .... "From the farm on the fens." An Old English "residence" name.

Ferdinand .... "Adventurous in life" (*Teutonic*). This has been a favorite royal name for nearly a thousand years.

Fergus .... "Of manly strength" (*Celtic*).

Fernald .... "Dweller by the old alder tree" (*Teutonic*).

Ferris .... "A rock." A Celtic form of Pierce, which, in turn, is derived from Peter.

Firman .... Probably "fair man" (*Old English*); but possibly from the Anglo-Saxon, meaning "traveler."

Fitzgerald .... "Son of Gerald" (*Teutonic*). Gerald means "mighty with the spear."

Fitzpatrick .... "Son of Patrick" (*Teutonic-Latin*). Patrick means "noble."

Fletcher .... "A fledger, or featherer, of arrows" (*Teutonic*). An "occupation" name.

Florian .... "Flowering" (*Latin*).

Floyd .... "The gray" (*Celtic*).

Forrest .... "Woodland dweller" (*Anglo-Latin*).

Foster .... "Keeper of the forest, or forester" (*Anglo-Latin*).

Fowler .... "Bird-catcher" or "game-keeper" (*Old English*).

Francis .... "Free" (*Teutonic*). From the Germanic tribe of Franks who called themselves "the free," and later gave their name to France. As a personal name it originated with St. Francis of Assisi, whose baptismal name was Giovanni, but who, after a journey into France, was nicknamed Francesco.

153

Frank .... Short for Francis, but often used as an independent name.

Franklin .... "A freeman or freeholder" (*Teutonic*).

Frayne .... Derivation doubtful; probably "foreigner" (*Old English*).

Fred .... Short for Frederick, but also used as an independent name.

Frederick, Frederic .... "Peaceful ruler" (*Teutonic*). The first syllable of this name can be traced back to the Teutonic goddess who gave her name to Friday. It is used in every European language, and no king of Prussia has ruled without it. DIM. Fred, Freddy.

Freeland .... "From the free land" (*Old English*). A "residence" name.

Freeman .... "A freeman"—or one who has acquired the rights of a citizen (*Anglo-Saxon*).

Fritz .... "Peaceful ruler" (*Teutonic*). A German form of Frederick.

G

Gabriel .... "God is my strength" (*Hebrew*). The Archangel of the Annunciation.

Gail, Gale .... "Gay or lively" (*Old English*). This is the most probable derivation of this name, although it may be traced to other sources.

Galen .... A name made famous by Galen, the Greek physician and philosopher. The meaning is unknown.

Galvin .... "Sparrow" (*Celtic*). A "bird" name, like Swan or Drake.

Gamaliel .... "God is my rewarder or judge" (*Hebrew*).

Gardell .... "A guardian or watchman" (*Teutonic*).

Gardener, Gardiner .... "A gardener" (*Teutonic*). An "occupation" name.

Garland .... "Crowned for victory" or "garlanded" (*Old French*).

Garner .... "Protecting warrior" (*Teutonic*).

Garrett .... "Mighty with the spear" (*Teutonic*).

Garrick .... "Spear king" (*Teutonic*).

Garvin .... "Befriending warrior" (*Teutonic*).

Gaston .... A form of Gascon, meaning "a native of Gascony."

Geoffrey .... A form of Godfrey, meaning "God's peace" (*Teutonic*).

George .... "Farmer or husbandman" (*Greek*); literally "tiller of the soil." Although St. George is England's patron saint the name was uncommon in English before 1700. Since then it has become one of the most popular names in England and in America.

Gerald .... "Mighty with the spear" (*Teutonic*).

Gerard .... "Brave with the spear" (*Teutonic*).

Gerry .... Short for Gerald, above.

Gersham, Gershom .... "The expelled or exiled" (*Hebrew*).

Gifford .... Literally "gift-brave" (*Teutonic*), so perhaps "splendid gift." Also a Norman-French nickname meaning "chubby-cheeked."

Gilbert, Gilburt .... "Illustrious pledge, or hostage" (*Teutonic*).

Giles .... "Bearer of the shield" (*Greek*). St. Giles is patron saint of the poor.

Gilford .... "From Gill's ford" (*Old English*). The name Gill was an Old French contraction of Julius.

Gilfred .... "Pledge of peace" (*Teutonic*).

Gilmer .... "Famous hostage" (*Teutonic*).

Gilmore .... "Servant of Mary"—namely, the Virgin Mary (*Celtic*).

Gilroy .... "Servant of the king" (*Celtic-Latin*), or "servant of the red-haired lord" (*Celtic*).

Gladwin .... "Cheerful friend" (*Old English*).

Glen, Glenn .... "Of the glen or valley" (*Gaelic*). A "residence" name.

Glendon .... "From the dark valley or glen" (*Gaelic*). A "residence" name.

Goddard .... "Divinely firm" (*Teutonic*).

Godfrey .... "God's peace" (*Teutonic*).

Godwin, Goodwin .... "Divine friend" (*Teutonic*).

Gordon .... "From the three-cornered hill." An Old English "residence" name.

Graham .... "From the gray house or home" (*Teutonic*). A "residence" name.

Grant .... "Great" (*Latin*).

Grantham .... "From the great meadow" (*Old English*). A "residence" name.

Grantland, Grantley .... "From the large place, or meadow" (*Latin-Old English*). A "residence" name.

Granville, Grenville .... "From the large town." An Old French "residence" name.

Grayson .... "Son of the reeve or bailiff" (*Old English*). A reeve was the chief magistrate of a town or district.

Gregory .... "Watchman" (*Greek*). A name assumed by seventeen Popes.

Gresham .... "From the grazing, or grass, land." An Old English "residence" name.

Griswold .... "From the gray forest or wold" (*Teutonic*). A "residence" name. But it may also mean "from the wild swine forest."

Grosvenor .... "Mighty huntsman" (*French-Latin*).

Grover .... "Dweller in the grove" (*Old English*).

Gustavus, Gustave .... "Staff of the Goths" (*Teutonic*). The Goths were an ancient Germanic race whose name has been interpreted as "noble."

Guthrie .... A Celtic name of obscure origin; perhaps from Guthrum, an early Danish king who invaded England and whose name signified "war serpent."

Guy .... A name of several possible derivations with different meanings. Either "sensible" (*Celtic*), "guide" (*Old French*), "warrior" (*Teutonic*), or "life" (*Latin*). The reader may take his choice.

H

Hadden, Hadden .... "From the heath or moor" (*Old English*). A "residence" name.

Hadley .... "From the heath-covered meadow." An Old English "residence" name.

Hadwin .... "Friend in war" (*Teutonic*).

Haines .... "Dweller in the hedged enclosure" (*Teutonic*).

Hal .... Short for either Henry or Harold, but also used as an independent name.

Halbert .... "Bright stone, or gem" (*Teutonic*).

Halden .... "Half-Dane" (*Teutonic*). From Halfdan, a pirate of mixed blood, who invaded England in King Alfred's time.

Hale .... Either "dweller at the hall," an Old English "residence" name; or possibly "robust" (*Teutonic*).

Halford .... "From the hall, or manor, by the ford" (*Old English*). A "residence" name.

Hall .... "From the hall or manor." An Old English "residence" name.

Hallam .... "From the hillside" (*Teutonic*). A "residence" name.

Halsey .... An Old English "residence" name meaning "from Hal's island." See Hal, above.

Hamilton .... A Norman name, possibly signifying "from the beautiful mountain."

Hamlin .... An early Norman form of Henry, meaning "ruler of the home" (*Teutonic*).

Hanford .... "From the high ford" (*Old English*). A "residence" name.

Hanley .... "From the high meadow." An Old English "residence" name.

Hans .... A short form of Johannes, or John, meaning "God's gracious gift" (*Hebrew*).

Hansel .... A Bavarian form of John. See Hans.

Harcourt .... A French "residence" name compounded from the Teutonic "fortified" and the Old French "court or dwelling."

Harden .... "From the hare valley" (*Old English*). A "residence" name.

Hardy, Hardie .... "Strong or hardy" (*Teutonic*).

Harlan, Harland .... "From the land of warriors" (*Teutonic*).

Harley .... "From the hare meadow," or possibly "the stags' meadow" (*Old English*). A "residence" name.

Harold .... "Mighty in battle" (*Teutonic*). DIM. Hal, Harry.

Harris .... "Son of Harry."

Harry .... Short for either Henry (which see), or for Harold.

Hartley .... "From the stags' meadow" (*Old English*). A "residence" name.

Hartwell .... "From the deers' spring or well" (*Teutonic*). A "residence" name.

 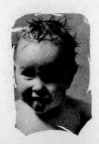

Harvey .... Possibly from "Houerv," an ancient bard of Brittany whose name meant "bitter."

Hayden, Haydon .... "From the hedged hill or down" (*Teutonic*). A "residence" name.

Hayes .... "From the hedged place" (*Old English*). A "residence" name.

Heath .... "From the heath, or waste-land." An Old English "residence" name.

Hector .... "Steadfast" (*Greek*). The Trojan hero of Homer's "Iliad."

Henry .... "Ruler of the home" (*Teutonic*). A favorite name, borne as Heinrich by six Germanic emperors and innumerable princes, and transmitted to the royal houses of France and England. The original English form was Harry, Henry being an imitation of Henri, the French spelling. DIM. Harry, Hal.

Herbert .... "Bright warrior" (*Teutonic*). DIM. Bert.

Herman .... "War man or warrior" (*Teutonic*).

Herwin .... "Friend, or lover, of war" (*Teutonic*).

Hezekiah .... "God is my strength" (*Hebrew*).

Hilary, Hillary, Hillery .... "Cheerful" (*Latin*).

Hilliard .... "Guardian in war" (*Teutonic*).

Hilton .... "From the manor on the hill" (*Old English*). A "residence" name.

Hiram .... "Exalted" (*Hebrew*).

Hobart .... "Bright-minded" (*Teutonic*). A form of Hubert.

Holbrook .... "From the brook in the dale." An Old English "residence" name.

Holden .... Probably "kindly or gracious" (*Teutonic*).

Hollis .... "Dweller by the holly trees" (*Old English*). A "residence" name.

Holman .... "From the river island" (*Teutonic*). A "residence" name.

Holmes .... "Son of Holman." See above.

Homer .... "A pledge or security" (*Greek*). The name of the ancient Greek poet credited with the authorship of the "Iliad" and "Odyssey."

Horace, Horatio .... "Keeper of the hours, or time-keeper" (*Latin*).

Hosea .... "Salvation" (*Hebrew*).

Howard .... "Chief warden or guardian" (*Teutonic*).

Howland .... "From the hilly land" (*Old English*). A "residence" name.

Hubert .... "Bright-minded" (*Teutonic*). St. Hubert is the patron saint of hunters and sportsmen.

Hugh, Hugo .... "Intelligent" (*Teutonic*).

Humphrey, Humfrey .... "Prop, or supporter, of peace" (*Teutonic*).

Hunt, Hunter .... "Huntsman" (*Old English*).

Huntley .... "From the hunter's meadow." An Old English "residence" name.

Hyman .... A variant of Hyam, meaning "life" (*Hebrew*).

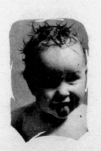 

WHAT SHALL WE NAME THE BABY?

I

Ian .... "God's gracious gift" (*Hebrew*). A Scotch form of John.

Ichabod .... "The glory has departed" (*Hebrew*).

Iden .... "Prosperous" (*Anglo-Saxon*).

Ignatius, Ignace .... "Ardent or fiery" (*Latin*).

Ingram .... "Ing's raven" (*Teutonic*). Ing was a mythical Scandinavian hero.

Innis, Inness .... "From the island" (*Celtic*). A "residence" name.

Ira .... "Descendant" (*Hebrew*).

Irvin .... A "residence" name from the Irvine River, Scotland. The word "irvine" means either "the white," or "the west" (*Celtic*).

Irving .... Same as Irvin, above.

Irwin .... "Lover of the sea" (*Anglo-Saxon*).

Isaac, Izaak .... "He who laughs, or the laugher" (*Hebrew*). Isaac was a Hebrew patriarch and the son of Abraham.

Isaiah .... "Salvation of the Lord" (*Hebrew*). The greatest of the Hebrew prophets.

Isidore, Isadore .... Probably meaning "gift of Isis" (*Greek*). Isis was the Egyptian goddess of the moon.

Israel .... "Soldier for the Lord" (*Hebrew*). This became the national name of the twelve Hebrew tribes.

Ivan .... "God's gracious gift" (*Hebrew*). A Russian form of John.

Iver, Ivar .... "Army bowman or archer" (*Scandinavian*).

J

Jack .... Properly a short form of Jacob; but in modern use more commonly a diminutive of John.

Jacob .... "The supplanter" (*Hebrew*). The ancestor of the ten tribes of Israel. DIM. Jack, Jake, Jock.

James .... "The supplanter" (*Hebrew*). Originally a form of Jacob. One of the disciples and an apostle. St. James the Apostle is the patron saint of Spain. DIM. Jim, Jem, Jimmy, Jamie.

Jared .... "The descending, or descendant" (*Hebrew*). See Jordan, which comes from the same word.

Jarvis .... "Keen as the spear" (*Teutonic*).

Jason .... "The healer" (*Greek*). A legendary hero of Greek mythology.

Jasper .... Either a form of Caspar (which see); or from the "jasper," a precious stone worn in the breastplate of the Hebrew high priest.

Jay .... A "bird" nickname, which in Old German means "the quick, or lively."

Jed .... Either a contraction of Jedidiah, meaning "beloved of the Lord" (*Hebrew*); or "The Hand," the Arabic name of a star.

Jeffrey .... A form of Geoffrey, which in turn is a form of Godfrey, meaning "God's peace" (*Teutonic*).

Jeremiah, Jeremy .... "Appointed, or exalted of the Lord" (*Hebrew*). Jeremiah was the second of the greater Biblical prophets. DIM. Jerry.

Jerome .... 'Of sacred name" (*Greek*).

Jerrold .... "Mighty with the spear" (*Teutonic*). A form of Gerald.

Jesse .... Either "grace, or gift, of God," or "rich" (*Hebrew*).

Job .... "The persecuted" (*Hebrew*). Hero of the Biblical Book of Job.

Joel .... "Jehovah is God" (*Hebrew*). One of the Biblical prophets.

John .... "God's gracious gift" (*Hebrew*). The "beloved disciple" of the New Testament. This favorite name has ninety-three variant forms used in twenty-seven different languages. DIM. Jack, Johnny, Jock.

Johnston .... A Scotch form of Johnson, or "son of John."

Jonas .... A form of Jonah, which means "dove" (*Hebrew*).

Jonathan .... "Gift of the Lord" (*Hebrew*).

Jordan .... "The descender" (*Hebrew*). From the river in Palestine which "descends" into the Dead Sea.

Joseph .... When the Hebrew patriarch Joseph was born, his triumphant mother said, "The Lord shall add to me another son" (Genesis xxx:24), and she called his name Joseph which means in Hebrew "He shall add." The name now usually commemorates St. Joseph, the husband of the Virgin Mary.

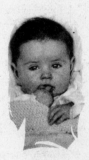

Joshua .... "Whose salvation is the Lord" (*Hebrew*). DIM. Josh.

Josiah .... "Yielded to the Lord" or "the Lord healeth" (*Hebrew*).

Jules .... A French form of Julius, below.

Julian .... A form of Julius, below.

Julius .... "Downy-bearded, or youthful" (*Greek*). A name made famous by Julius Caesar. For its origin see the Foreword.

Junius .... "Youthful" (*Latin*). Sometimes used for a child born in the month of June.

Justin .... "The just, or upright" (*Latin*).

K

Kane, Kayne .... "Fair or bright" (*Celtic*).

Karl .... A German form of Charles, which see.

Karsten .... "The Christian, or anointed" (*Greek*). A Slavonic form of Christian.

Keane, Keene .... Either "sharp" (*Old English*), or "tall," "handsome" (*Celtic*).

Keegan, Kegan .... A contraction of MacEgan, or "Son of Egan." Egan means "the fiery" (*Celtic*).

Keir .... "Dark-skinned" (*Celtic*).

Keith .... A name of uncertain origin, perhaps from a Welsh surname meaning "wood-dweller."

Kelby .... "From the farm by the spring" (*Teutonic*). A "residence" name.

Kelsey, Kelcey .... "Dweller by the water" (*Teutonic*).

Kelvin, Kelwin .... "From the narrow river." A Celtic "residence" name.

Kendall, Kendal .... "From the bright valley" (*Celtic*). A "residence" name.

Kenley .... "From the king's meadow" (*Old English*). A "residence" name.

Kenneth .... "Comely" (*Celtic*).

Kenric, Kendrick .... "Bold, or royal, ruler" (*Anglo-Saxon*).

Kent .... Probably from the English county of Kent, which in Celtic signifies "white or bright."

Kenton .... "From a farmstead in Kent." A "residence" name.

Kenway .... "Courageous in battle" (*Anglo-Saxon*).

Kenyon .... "White, or blond-haired" (*Gaelic*).

Kermit .... Originally Kermode, a contraction of Mac-Dermott, which signifies "son of Diarmaid." Diarmaid means "god of arms" (*Celtic*).

Kerry, Keary .... Probably from the Irish county of Kerry, which means "the dark" (*Celtic*).

Kerwin, Kirwin .... "Dark-skinned" (*Celtic*).

Kester .... Either "of the Roman camp" (*Latin*), or a short form of Christopher, "Christ-bearer" (*Greek*).

Kevin .... "Kind or gentle" (*Celtic*).

Kilby .... "From the farmstead by the spring" (*Teutonic*). A "residence" name.

Kilian .... A Celtic form of Cecil, "blind" (*Latin*).

Kim .... Possibly meaning "chief" (*Welsh*).

Kimball .... "Royally brave" (*Anglo-Saxon*).

Kingdon .... "From the king's hill." An Old English "residence" name.

Kingsley .... "From the king's meadow" (*Old English*). A "residence" name.

Kingston .... "From the king's manor." An Old English "residence" name.

Kirby, Kerby .... "From the church, or kirk, village" (*Teutonic*). A "residence" name.

Kirk .... "Dweller by the church" (*Teutonic*). A "residence" name.

Kit .... Short for Christopher, meaning "the Christ-bearer" (*Greek*).

Konrad .... A German form of Conrad, meaning "able in counsel" (*Teutonic*).

Kurt .... A German diminutive of Konrad, above.

L

Laban .... "White" (*Hebrew*).

Lambert .... Literally "land bright" (*Teutonic*); so perhaps meaning "glory of his country."

Lamont .... "Lawyer" (*Scandinavian*). An "occupation" name.

Landers, Landis .... "From the grassy plain, or lawn" (*Old French*). A "residence" name.

Landon, Langdon .... "From the long hill." An Old English "residence" name.

Landry .... "Ruler of the place," or "local magnate" (*Anglo-Saxon*).

Lane .... "From the lane, or rural road" (*Old English*). A "residence" name.

Lang .... "Long" or "tall" (*Teutonic*).

Langley .... Probably an Old English "residence" name meaning "from the long meadow." But perhaps from the Old French "l'anglais," meaning "Englishman."

Lars, Larz .... Swedish and Danish contractions of Lawrence, which see.

Latham .... "Dweller by the barns" (*Teutonic*). A "residence" name.

Lathrop .... A name of obscure origin, though the "throp" or "thorp" signifies "village" in Anglo-Saxon.

Latimer .... Originally "Latiner," or interpreter of Latin (*Anglo-French*). An "occupation" name.

Launcelot, Lancelot .... "One who serves" (*Latin*). A famous knight in the King Arthur legends.

Lawrence, Laurence .... "The laurel" (*Latin*). Sacred to the Greek god Apollo, the laurel was supposed to inspire prophecy and poetry (compare "poet laureate"); and, as the winners in ancient games were crowned with laurel wreaths, it became also the symbol of victory. DIM. Larry, Laurie.

Lawton .... "From the hillside farm" (*Old English*). A "residence" name.

Leal .... "Faithful" (*Old French-Latin*).

Leander .... "Lion-man" or "courageous" (*Greek*).

Learoyd .... "From the cleared meadow" (*Teutonic*). A "residence" name.

Ledyard .... Perhaps a corrupt form of Leger, the name of a famous French saint of the seventh century; or from the surname Ledgard, which means "the nation's guardian" (*Teutonic*).

Lee .... This may, with equally good authority, mean "lion" (*Latin*), "meadow-dweller" (*Old English*), "a shelter" (*Old English*), "physician" (*Celtic*), or "gray" (*Celtic*).

Leigh .... "Dweller in the lea, or meadow" (*Old English*).

Leighton .... Either "from the meadow farm" or "from the herb-garden" (*Old English*). A "residence" name.

Leith .... A name derived from the River Leith in Scotland. The word "leith" means "wide" (*Celtic*).

Leland .... "From the meadow land" (*Old English*). A "residence" name.

Lemuel .... "Dedicated to God" (*Hebrew*).

Leo .... "The lion" (*Latin*). A name assumed by thirteen Popes.

Leon .... "The lion, or lion-like" (*French-Latin*).

Leonard .... "Brave, or strong, as the lion" (*Teutonic*).

Leopold .... "Bold for the people" or "patriotic" (*Teutonic*).

Leroy .... "Royal" (*Old French-Latin*).

Leslie .... "From the gray fort" (*Celtic*). A "residence" name.

Lester, Leicester .... Derived from the English town of Leicester, the name of which probably means "camp of the legion" (*Latin*).

Levi .... "United" (*Hebrew*).

Lew .... Either a Slavonic form of Lionel, meaning "lion-like" (*Latin*); or "refuge" (*Old English*).

Lincoln .... "From the settlement by the pool" (*Celtic-Latin*). A "residence" name.

Lindley .... "From the linden tree meadow" (*Old English*). A "residence" name.

Lindsay, Lindsey .... Perhaps meaning "from the island of serpents" (*Teutonic*). A "residence" name.

Lionel .... "Lion-like" (*Latin*).

Livingston .... An Old English "residence" name signifying "from Lyfing's place." Lyfing was a proper name which means "beloved son."

Llewellyn .... Either "lion-like" or "ruler" (*Celtic*).

Lloyd .... "Gray" (*Celtic*).

Lockwood .... "From the enclosed wood" (*Old English*). A "residence" name.

Lombard .... "Long-beard" (*Teutonic*). The Lombards (long-beards) of Italy were famous bankers. Lombard Street, in London's financial district, took its name from them.

Lorenzo .... An Italian form of Lawrence, which see.

Lorimer, Lorrimer .... "Harness-maker" (*Latin*). An "occupation" name.

Lorin, Loren, Lauren .... Forms of Lawrence, which see.

Loring .... A name derived from the French duchy of Lorraine. Lorraine means "famous in war" (*Old High German*).

Lot .... "Veiled" (*Hebrew*).

Louis, Lewis .... "Famous in battle" (*Teutonic*). This name, originally Hludwig and later Clovis, was borne by several ancient Frankish kings. It was latinized as Ludovicus; and in the shorter French form of Louis was used by no less than eighteen French kings. It has always, in both spellings, been popular in English.

Lowell .... A form of Lovell, which means "beloved" (*Old English*).

Lucien, Lucian .... Forms of Lucius, below.

Lucius .... "Light" (*Latin*). A favorite name for a child born at daybreak.

Ludlow .... "From the prince's hill" (*Old English*). A "residence" name.

Luke, Lucas .... "Light" (*Latin*). St. Luke was the author of the third Biblical Gospel.

Luther .... "Famous warrior" (*Teutonic*). Commemorates the German monk Martin Luther, who led the Reformation.

Lydell .... "From the wide, or open, dell" (*Old English*). A "residence" name.

Lyle, Lisle .... "From the island." A French-Latin "residence" name.

Lyman .... "Man from the valley" (*Old English*).

Lyndon .... "From the linden tree hill" (*Teutonic*). A "residence" name.

Lynn, Linn .... "Dweller by the torrent or cascade" (*Anglo-Saxon*).

Lysander .... "Liberator" (*Greek*).

M

Mac .... A Celtic prefix meaning "son of." For example, MacArthur, or McArthur, means "son of Arthur," etc.

Macklin .... Originally MacFlann, or "son of Flann." Flann in Celtic means "red-haired."

Macnair .... "Son of the heir" (*Gaelic*).

Maddox, Maddock .... "Beneficent" (*Celtic*).

Madison .... Possibly "son of Maud." Maud is a form of Matilda, which means "mighty in battle" (*Teutonic*).

Magnus .... "Great" (*Latin*).

Maitland .... "From the meadow-land (*Old English*). A "residence" name.

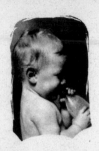 

Malcolm .... "Servant of Columba" (*Celtic*). St. Columba was a sixth-century Scotch missionary. His name means "the dove" (*Latin*).

Mallory .... "Ill-omened" (*Old French-Latin*).

Malvin, Melvin .... "Servant" or "chief" (*Celtic*). The root-word may have either meaning.

Mandel .... Perhaps originally Mantel, an Old French "occupation" name for a maker of cloaks or garments.

Manton .... "From Mann's estate" (*Anglo-Saxon*). Mann was the equivalant of "king's man," or vassal—namely, one who held land direct from the king.

Manuel .... Short for Emmanuel, meaning "God with us" (*Hebrew*).

Manvel, Manvil .... "From the great estate" (*Latin*). A "residence" name.

Marcus .... The original form of Mark, which see.

Mardon, Marden .... "From the valley with the pool" (*Old English*). A "residence" name.

Mario .... An Italian form of Marius, below.

Marius .... "Martial." From Mars, the Latin god of war.

Mark, Marc .... Marcus, from which these forms come, is an ancient Latin name, perhaps meaning "hammer"; perhaps derived from Mars, the god of war.

Marland .... "From the boundary, or mark land" (*Old English*). A "residence" name.

WHAT SHALL WE NAME THE BABY?

Marlow .... "From the hill by the lake." An Old English "residence" name.

Marsden .... "From the marsh valley" (*Old English*). A "residence" name.

Marshall, Marshal .... "A marshal" (*Old French*). Marshals were originally officers in charge of horses.

Marston .... "From the farm by the pool." An Old English "residence" name.

Martin .... "The warlike." From Mars, the Latin god of war.

Marvin, Marwin .... "Famous friend," or "sea-friend" (*Teutonic*).

Mason .... "A mason," or worker in stone (*French-Teutonic*). An "occupation" name.

Mathias, Mattias .... Forms of Matthew, below.

Matthew .... "Gift of God" (*Hebrew*). St. Matthew was one of the twelve apostles. DIM. Mat.

Maurice .... "Moorish" or "dark-skinned" (*Latin*).

Max .... A short form of Maximilian, below, but used as an individual name.

Maximilian .... "The greatest" (*Latin*).

Maxwell .... An Anglo-Saxon "residence" name, signifying "from Maccus' spring, or pool." Maccus was some ancient Celtic gentleman whose name was a form of Marcus.

Maynard .... "Mightily brave" (*Teutonic*).

Medwin .... "Powerful friend" (*Teutonic*).

Meldon .... "From the hillside mill" (*Old English*). A "residence" name.

Melville .... Either a form of Malvin, which see; or a "place" name from Malleville, Normandy.

Mercer .... "Merchant" (*French-Latin*). An "occupation" name. A mercer was originally a dealer in any kind of merchandise.

Meredith, Meridith .... An Old Welsh name of uncertain meaning. Perhaps "protector from the sea."

Merlin .... The name of the enchanter in the legends of King Arthur. It may mean "from the sea-girt hill" (*Celtic*), or be a "bird" name from the merlin, a falcon used in hawking (*Old French-Latin*).

Merrell, Merrill .... "Famous" (*Teutonic*).

Merrick .... Shortened from the Teutonic Almeric, which means "industrious ruler."

Merton .... "From the farm by the sea" (*Anglo-Saxon*).

Merwin, Merwyn .... "Lover, or friend, of the sea" (*Teutonic*).

Micah .... "Like unto the Lord" (*Hebrew*). One of the minor Hebrew prophets.

Michael .... "Like unto the Lord" (*Hebrew*). Michael was an archangel, and chief of the angelic host. DIM. Mike.

Milburn .... "From the mill stream" (*Old English*). A "residence" name.

Miles, Myles .... Either "soldier" (*Latin*); or "the mill or crusher" (*Greek*).

Miller .... "A miller" (*Latin*). An "occupation" name.

Millman, Milman .... "Man of the mill" (*Old English-Latin*).

Milton .... "From the mill farmstead" (*Old English*). Surname of John Milton, the famous English poet.

Milward .... "Keeper of the mill" (*Old English-Latin*).

Mitchell .... A form of Michael, above.

Montague .... "Of the peaked mountain" (*Latin*). A "residence" name.

Moreland .... Either "from the moor," or "from the land of the Moors" (*Old English*).

Morgan .... "Born by the sea" (*Celtic*).

Morley .... "From the meadow on the moor" (*Old English*). A "residence" name.

Morrell, Morel .... "Swarthy" (*Latin*).

Morris .... "Moorish" or "dark-skinned" (*Latin*).

Mortimer .... "Dweller by the still water" (*French-Latin*).

Morton .... "From the farm, or village, on the moor" (*Old English*). A "residence" name.

Morven .... "Mariner" (*Celtic*).

Moses .... "Drawn from the water" (*Greek*). The Biblical Moses, who was "drawn from the water" by Pharoah's daughter, led the Jews out of bondage and became their lawgiver. DIM. Mose, Moe.

Moulton .... "From the mule farm" (*Old English-Latin*). A "residence" name.

Munro, Munroe, Monroe .... "From the red marsh" (*Latin*). A "residence" name.

Murdock .... "Prosperous seaman" (*Celtic*).

Murray, Murry .... "Seaman" (*Celtic*).

N

Nahum .... "The compassionate, or comforter" (*Hebrew*). A minor Biblical prophet.

Naldo .... A Spanish contraction of Ronald, which means "of mighty, or wise, power" (*Teutonic*).

Nathan .... A shorter form of Nathaniel, below.

Nathaniel .... "Gift of the Lord" (*Hebrew*). DIM. Nat, Nate.

Neal, Neil .... "Chief or champion" (*Celtic*).

Nealon .... A form of Neal, above.

Nehemiah .... "Comforted by the Lord" (*Hebrew*).

Nelson .... "Son of Neal." Also occasionally used for "the son of Nell."

Nestor .... The oldest and wisest of the Greek chieftains at the siege of Troy. Hence the name implies "wisdom."

Neville .... "From the new town" (*Latin*). A "residence" name.

Nevin .... "Nephew" (*Teutonic*).

Newlin, Newlyn .... "From the new spring or pool" (*Celtic*). A "residence" name.

Newton .... "From the new estate or farmstead." An Anglo-Saxon "residence" name, made famous by Sir Isaac Newton, the English scientist.

Nicholas, Nicolas .... "The people's victory" (*Greek*). Saint Nicholas is the patron saint of children. DIM. Nick, Nicol.

Nicodemus .... "Conqueror of, or victorious over, the people" (*Greek*).

Nigel .... "Dark" (*Latin*).

Niles .... A form, originally Finnish, of Nicholas, above.

Noah .... "Rest" (*Hebrew*), although the Biblical patriarch Noah led a far from restful life.

Noel .... "Christmas" (*French-Latin*). A name often given to a child born at Christmastide.

Nolan, Noland .... "Noble, or famous" (*Celtic*).

Norbert .... "Njord's brightness" or "brightness of the sea" (*Teutonic*). Njord was the god of sailors in Norse mythology.

Norman .... "Man from the north" (*Teutonic*), or a Norman.

Norris .... Either "man from the north" (*Teutonic*); or "caretaker" if from the Old French-Latin.

Norton .... "From the north farmstead or village" (*Anglo-Saxon*). A "residence" name.

Norval .... A name, probably invented by John Home in his popular play "Douglas" (1757), for a Scotch shepherd.

Norvin .... Perhaps "man from the north" (*Teutonic*).

Norward .... "Guardian of the northern road or gate" (*Teutonic*).

O

Oakes .... "The oak." An Old English "tree" name.

Oakley .... "From the oak tree meadow" (*Old English*). A "residence" name.

Obadiah .... "Servant of the Lord" (*Hebrew*). One of the minor Hebrew prophets. DIM. Obed.

Octavius .... "The eighth born" (*Latin*). A name made world-famous by Octavius Caesar, the first Roman emperor.

Odell .... Either "man of property" (*Norse*), or "of the dale, or valley" (*Old English*).

Ogden .... Originally Oakden, or "from the oak tree valley." An Old English "residence" name.

Olaf .... King Olaf christianized Norway and became its patron saint. The name means "relic, or reminder, of his ancestor" (*Old Norse*).

Olin, Olen .... Perhaps derived from the name Olaf, above.

Oliver .... "The olive" (*Latin*), betokening "peace." The olive, sacred to the Greek goddess Athene, came to signify peace, because the victors in athletic contests were crowned with olive wreaths; therefore to present an olive branch to the enemy marked the end of strife. In like manner, the olive leaf the dove bore to Noah in the ark betokened peace after the tempest of the flood. DIM. Noll, Ollie.

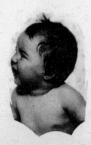

WHAT SHALL WE NAME THE BABY?

Olney .... An Old English "residence" name from the English town of Olney; but what the town's name signifies is unknown.

Olvan .... A form of Oliver, above.

Ordway .... "Warrior with spear" (*Anglo-Saxon*).

Orford .... "From the cattle ford" (*Old English*). A "residence" name.

Orin, Oran .... "White of skin" (*Celtic*).

Orland .... A form of Roland, meaning "fame of the land" (*Teutonic*).

Orlando .... An Italian form of Roland, which means "fame of the land" (*Teutonic*).

Ormond, Orman .... Probably "mariner, or ship man" (*Teutonic*). Literally "dragon man"; but, as the old Norse war-vessels had dragons for figureheads, the dragon came to signify "ship."

Orson .... Short for Orsino, which means "the bear" (*Latin*). The bear anciently typified strength.

Orton .... "Wealthy" (*Teutonic*).

Orville .... "Lord Orville" was the hero of Fanny Burney's highly popular novel "Evelina" (1779). She probably invented his name.

Orvin .... "Boar friend" (*Anglo-Saxon*); or, because the wild boar typified courage, "courageous friend."

Osborn .... "Divine bear" (*Teutonic*). As the bear was anciently respected for its strength, the name may be interpreted as "divinely strong."

Oscar .... "Leaping warrior" (*Celtic*).

Osgood .... "Divine creator" (*Teutonic*). "Os" was an ancient Norse divinity.

Osmond .... "Under divine protection" (*Teutonic*).

Osric .... "Divine ruler" (*Teutonic*).

Oswald .... "Of god-like power" (*Teutonic*).

Otis .... "Keen of hearing" (*Greek*).

Otto .... "Prosperous or wealthy" (*Teutonic*). A favorite name with ancient Germanic emperors.

Otway .... "Fortunate in battle" (*Teutonic*).

Outram .... "Prospering raven" (*Teutonic*). The raven was formerly the badge of a warrior. See Foreword.

Ovid .... Commemorates Ovid, the famous Roman poet.

Owen .... This name may come from three sources: "young warrior" (*Celtic*), "lamb" (*Celtic*), or "well-born" (*Greek*).

P

Page .... "Attendant on a noble" (*French*). An "occupation" name.

Paine, Payne .... "Man from the country, or a rustic" (*Latin*). As early Christianity was first preached in towns, the country-folk were called "pagan." In Old English this word was "payne."

Palmer .... "Palm-bearer." A "palmer" was a pilgrim to the Holy Land who returned bearing a palm-branch (*Old English-Latin*).

Park, Parke .... "Of the park, or enclosed woodland." An Old English "residence" name.

Parker .... "Keeper of the park" (*Old English*). An "occupation" name.

Pascal .... A name sometimes given to a child born during the Jewish Passover, or Christian Easter festival. Pascal literally means "pass over" (*Hebrew*).

Patrick .... "Noble or patrician" (*Latin*). St. Patrick is the patron saint of Ireland. DIM. Pat.

Paul .... "Little" (*Latin*). St. Paul, the New Testament apostle, spread the name through all Christian countries. It appears in twenty-two different forms.

Paxton, Paxon .... An "occupation" name derived from "pack man" or traveling trader (*Teutonic*).

Payton, Paton, Peyton .... Scotch diminutive forms of Patrick, above.

Pedro .... "A rock" (*Greek*). A Spanish and Portuguese form of Peter.

Pembroke .... "From the headland." An Old Welsh "residence" name.

Percival .... A name of uncertain origin. Perhaps originally from Perseus, "the destroyer," of Greek mythology, who slew the Gorgon. Possibly "the valley-piercer," or stalwart (*Old French-Latin*). Sir Percival was a knight of King Arthur's Round Table who searched for the Holy Grail.

Percy .... Short for Percival, above.

Perrin, Perren, Perryn .... Forms, through the French Pierre, of Peter, below.

Perry .... Either "the pear tree," an Old English "tree" name; or a form, through the French Pierre, of Peter, below.

Peter .... "A rock" (*Greek*). One of the twelve apostles, St. Peter is claimed by the Roman Catholic Church to be its first bishop or pope. DIM. Pete.

Phelan .... "Wolf" (*Celtic*). The wolf was anciently a highly respected animal. See the Foreword.

Philander .... "Lover of mankind" (*Greek*).

Philbert .... "Illustriously brilliant" (*Teutonic*).

Philip .... "Lover of horses" (*Greek*). One of the twelve apostles. "Horse lover" was a title borne by the ancient kings of Macedon, and inherited by Philip the Great. DIM. Phil.

Phineas .... "Oracle, or brazen mouth" (*Hebrew*).

Pierce, Pearce, Peirce .... Anglo-French forms of Peter, above.

Pierpont, Pierrepont .... "Dweller by the stone bridge" (*French-Latin*).

Pierre .... The usual French form of Peter, above.

Pierson, Pearson .... "Son of Pierre, or Peter." See Peter.

Pollard .... Either "the cropped-haired," a Teutonic nickname; or Paul with the added Teutonic adjective "ard," meaning "brave."

Porter .... "Keeper of the gate" (*Latin*). An "occupation" name.

Powell .... "Descendant of Howel." Howel was an ancient Welsh king, whose name probably means "the alert" (*Celtic*).

Prentice .... "An apprentice, or learner" (*Latin*). An "occupation" name.

Prescott .... "From the priest's dwelling" (*Old English*). A "residence" name.

Preston .... "From the domain of the church or priest." An Old English "residence" name.

Prince .... "Prince" (*Latin*). Later this became an Anglo-French title for an attendant upon a prince.

Prior, Pryor .... "A prior," or head of a monastery (*Latin*). Also an Old English and French title for a prior's servant.

Proctor .... "Manager or agent" (*Latin*). An "occupation" name.

Prosper .... "The fortunate" (*Latin*).

Putnam .... "Dweller by the pond or pit" (*Anglo-Saxon*). A "residence" name.

Q

Quentin .... "The fifth" (*Latin*). A name sometimes given to a fifth child, if a son.

Quinby .... "From the woman's estate" (*Scandinavian*). A "residence" name. Our word "queen" meant merely "woman or wife" in its old Teutonic form.

Quincy .... "From the place owned by the fifth son." An Old French-Latin "residence" name.

Quinn .... "The wise" (*Celtic*). A form of Conn.

R

Radburn, Radbourne .... "Dweller by the red stream." An Old English "residence" name.

Radcliffe .... "From the red cliff" (*Old English*). A "residence" name.

Radford .... "From the red ford" (*Old English*). A "residence" name.

Radley .... "From the red field, or meadow." An Old English "residence" name.

Raleigh .... "From the roe, or deer, meadow" (*Old English*). A "residence" name.

Ralph .... A short form of Randolph, below.

Ralston .... "From Ralph's estate." An Old English "residence" name.

Ramon .... A Spanish form of Raymond, which means "mighty protector" (*Teutonic*).

amsey, Ramsay .... "From Ram's island" (*Teutonic*). Ram was a personal name signifying either "the strong," "the raven," or "the ram."

andal, Randall .... Forms of Randolph, below.

andolph .... Either "house wolf" and so "protector"— the wolf anciently was esteemed for courage—or, from the emblem painted on a war shield, "shield wolf" (*Teutonic*).

aphael .... "Divine healer" (*Hebrew*). In Hebrew tradition Raphael was one of the four angels who stood about God's throne.

awdon .... "From the roe, or deer, hill" (*Teutonic*).

Ray .... Either "kingly" (*Old French*); or, more probably, short for Raymond, below.

Rayburn, Reyburn .... "From the roe, or deer, brook" (*Old English*). A "residence" name.

Raymond, Raymund .... "Mighty, or wise, protector" (*Teutonic*).

Read, Reed, Reid .... "Red-haired, or of ruddy complexion." An Old English nickname.

Redmund, Redmond .... "Adviser and protector" (*Teutonic*).

Regan .... "Kingly" (*Celtic*).

Reginald .... "Of mighty, or wise, power" (*Teutonic*). DIM. Reggie.

Remus .... The name of one of the traditional twin brothers, Remus and Romulus, who founded Rome.

WHAT SHALL WE NAME THE BABY?

Rendell .... A form of Randolph, which see.

Renfred .... "Peacemaker" (*Teutonic*).

Renwick .... Perhaps meaning "from the place where the ravens nest" (*Teutonic*). A "residence" name.

Reuben .... "Behold, a son!" (*Hebrew*). A name derived from his mother Leah's exclamation at his birth. Reuben founded the tribe of Israel which bore his name.

Rex .... "King" (*Latin*).

Rexford .... "From the king's ford" (*Latin-Old English*). A "residence" name.

Richard .... "Powerful ruler" (*Teutonic*). A favorite name with the Normans when they conquered England in 1066; and subsequently adopted in England as a popular and royal name. DIM. Dick.

Richmond .... "Mighty protector" (*Teutonic*).

Ridgley .... "Dweller at the meadow ridge" (*Old English*). A "residence" name.

Ridley .... "From the red field, or meadow" (*Old English*). A "residence" name.

Ripley .... "From the meadow belonging to Hrypa." Hrypa was an Anglo-Saxon name which meant "the shouter."

Robert .... "Of shining fame" (*Teutonic*). This name originated in Germany as Ruprecht, and first came to England from France. It is used in eight languages, and has some twenty different forms. DIM. Rob, Rab, Robin, Bob, Bobby.

Robin .... A form of Robert, made famous by Robin
Hood, the outlaw hero of English folklore.

Roderick, Rodrick, Roderic .... "Famous ruler" (*Teutonic*). DIM. Roddy.

Rodman .... Several meaning are possible: either "a rod
man, or measurer of land," or "dweller by the
rood or cross" (*Old English*); or "the red-haired"
(*Teutonic*).

Rodney .... "Famous" (*Teutonic*).

Roger .... "Famous spearman" (*Teutonic*).

Roland, Rowland .... "Fame of the land" (*Teutonic*).

Roldan .... A Spanish form of Roland, above.

Rolf, Rolfe, Rolph .... Shortened forms of Rudolph,
below; but also used as independent names.

Rollin .... A shortened form of Rudolph.

Rollo .... Like Rollin, a short form of Rudolph.

Romeo .... "A pilgrim to Rome" (*Italian-Latin*).

Romney .... Either a "residence" name from the English
town of Romney; or from the Latin, meaning "a
Roman."

Ronald .... "Of mighty power" (*Teutonic*). A contraction of Reginald.

Roscoe .... "From the roe, or deer, forest" (*Teutonic*).
A "residence" name.

Ross .... From an old Teutonic word meaning "horse."
The horse was the national emblem of the ancient
Saxons.

Roswell .... A form of Roswald, which means "mighty
steed" (*Teutonic*).

Roy .... Either "king" (*Old French*), or "red-haired"
(*Celtic*).

Royal .... "Kingly" (*Old French-Latin*).

Royce .... "Son of Roy, the kingly" (*Old French-Latin*).

Royd .... "From the forest clearing" (*Scandinavian*).
A "residence" name.

Royden .... Either "from the king's hill" (*French-Old
English*), or "from the hill where rye grows" (*Old
English*). A "residence" name.

187

Rudolph, Rudolf .... "Far-famed wolf" (*Teutonic*) DIM. Dolph, Rolf, Rolph, Rollin, Rollo.

Ruford .... "From the red ford" (*Old English*). A "residence" name.

Rufus ... "Red-haired" (*Latin*).

Rupert ... "Of shining fame" (*Teutonic*). Contracted from Ruprecht, which is the German form of Robert.

Russell .... Either "red-haired" (*Latin*); or "fox-like," for "russel" was the Old English name for the red fox.

Rutherford .... "From the cattle ford" (*Old English*). A "residence" name.

S

Sabin .... From the ancient Italian tribe of the Sabines, the meaning of whose name is lost.

Salisbury .... "From the fortified stronghold" (*Old English*); although another derivation suggests "dry town" (*Anglo-Saxon*).

Sam .... A short form either of Samuel or of Samson, below.

Samson, Sampson .... "Like the sun, or resplendent" (*Hebrew*); but suggesting "strength" from Samson, the strong man of the Bible.

Samuel .... "Asked of God" (*Hebrew*). A Biblical prophet.

Sanborn .... "From the sandy brook" (*Old English*). A "residence" name.

Sanders, Saunders .... "Son of Alexander." Alexander means "helper of mankind" (*Greek*).

Sandon .... "From the sandy hill." An Old English "residence" name.

Sandor .... Short for Alexander, which means "helper of mankind" (*Greek*).

Sanford .... "From the sandy ford" (*Old English*). A "residence" name.

Sargent .... "An officer, squire, or military attendant" (*Old French-Latin*). An "occupation" name.

Saul .... "Longed for" (*Hebrew*). A name borne by the first king of Israel; also the original name of the Apostle Paul.

Saville, Savill .... "From the willow farm" (*Old French-Latin*). A "residence" name.

Sawyer .... "A cutter of timber" (*Celtic*). An "occupation" name.

Saxon .... "A Saxon." From the Teutonic tribe which invaded England in the fifth century. Their name is generally interpreted as "swordsmen" from their short swords, though sometimes as "stone or rock."

Schuyler .... "A shelter" (*Dutch*).

Scot, Scott .... "A Scot, or Scotsman." The Scots were an Irish tribe who later settled Scotland. Their name probably means "tattooed," because they cut and painted their bodies; but is also interpreted as "the wanderers."

Seabrook .... "From the brook by the sea" (*Old English*). A "residence" name.

Seadon .... "From the hill by the sea." An Old English "residence" name.

Searle, Serle .... "Armed, or wearing armor" (*Teutonic*).

Seaton, Seton .... "From the place by the sea" (*Old English*). A "residence" name.

Seaver .... Probably originally Seber, meaning "victorious stronghold" (*Anglo-Saxon*).

Sebastian .... "The revered" (*Greek*).

Sefton .... From the town of Sefton, England; but what that ancient town's name signifies is obscure.

Selby .... "From the manor farm" (*Teutonic*). A "residence" name.

Seldon, Selden .... "From the manor valley" (*Teutonic*). A "residence" name.

Selwyn .... "Palace friend, or friend at court" (*Anglo-Saxon*).

Serge .... Short for Sergius, a favorite Roman and medieval name of unknown meaning. Especially popular in Russia from St. Sergius.

Seth .... "The appointed" (*Hebrew*). Seth was the third son of Adam.

Severin .... Probably from the river Severn in England. Compare the feminine Sabrina.

Seward .... "Guardian of the seacoast" (*Anglo-Saxon*).

Sewell .... Either "mighty at sea," or "mighty in victory" (*Teutonic*).

Seymour .... If of French origin it comes from St. Maur, or "the Moorish saint" (*French-Latin*). If from the Teutonic it means "famed at sea." It may also signify "tailor" (*Old English*).

Shaw .... "From the shady grove." An Old English "residence" name.

Shawn .... "God's gracious gift" (*Hebrew*). An Irish form of John.

Shelby .... "From the ledge farm" (*Anglo-Saxon*). A "residence" name.

Sheldon .... "From the hill on the ledge" (*Anglo-Saxon*). A "residence" name.

Shelley .... "From the ledge meadow" (*Anglo-Saxon*). A surname often used as a given name by admirers of the English poet Shelley.

Shepherd, Shepard .... "A shepherd" (*Anglo-Saxon*). An "occupation" name.

Shepley .... "From the sheep meadow, or grazing ground" (*Anglo-Saxon*). A "residence" name.

Sherard .... "Of splendid valor" (*Anglo-Saxon*).

Sheridan .... An ancient Irish nickname, meaning "the wild man" (*Celtic*).

Sherlock .... "Fair-haired" (*Old English*).

Sherman .... "A shearer, or cutter, of the nap of woolen cloth" (*Old English*). An "occupation" name.

Sherwin .... Either the Old English nickname for a swift runner, that is, "one who cuts the wind"; or "eminent in friendship" (*Anglo-Saxon*).

Sherwood .... "From the bright forest" (*Old English*). Sherwood Forest in England is famous as the haunt of the legendary outlaw, Robin Hood.

Sibley .... Meaning "prophetic" if derived from Sibyl, the prophetess of Latin mythology. If from the Anglo-Saxon it means "the friendly or related."

Sidney, Sydney .... Either derived from Sidon, the oldest city of ancient Phoenicia; or from the French St. Denys. Compare the feminine Sidonia.

Sidwell .... An English form of St. Sativola, an ancient Celtic martyr. Or perhaps a "residence" name meaning "from the broad well" (*Old English*).

Siegfried, Sigfrid .... "Victorious peace" (*Teutonic*). The hero of the ancient German Nibelungen legends.

Sigmund .... "Victorious protection" (*Teutonic*).

Silas .... "Man of the forest" (*Latin*). From Silvanus, below.

Silsby .... "From Sill's farm." An Old English "residence" name. "Sill" was a common contraction of Silvester.

Silvanus, Sylvanus .... "Forest-dweller" (*Latin*). Silvanus was the Roman god of forests, flocks and herds.

Silvester, Sylvester .... "Forest-dweller" (*Latin*).

Simeon, Simon .... "Heard" (*Hebrew*). In the Biblical narrative (Genesis xxix:33), Leah called her son Simeon because she said, "The Lord hath *heard*." DIM. Sim.

Simpson, Simson .... "The son of Sim," which is short for Simon or Simeon, above. Simson is also a Swedish form of Samson.

Sinclair .... A contracted, and male, form of Saint Claire. Claire means "the illustrious" (*Latin*).

Sloan, Sloane .... "Warrior" (*Celtic*).

Sol .... "The sun" (*Latin*). Sol was the sun-god of Roman mythology. The name is also a short form of Solomon, below.

Solomon .... "Peaceful" (*Hebrew*); but as the name commemorates the Biblical King Solomon, renowned for his wisdom, it has come to signify "the wise."

Spencer, Spenser .... "Keeper, or dispenser, of provisions" (*Old English-Latin*). An "occupation" name.

Sprague .... "Alert or lively" (*Teutonic*).

Stacey, Stacy .... "Stable or dependable" (*Latin*). Also a contraction of Anastasius.

Stafford .... "From the landing ford" (*Old English*). A "residence" name.

Standish .... "From the stony park, or enclosure." An Old English "residence" name.

Stanfield .... "From the stony field" (*Old English*). A "residence" name.

Stanford .... "From the stoned, or paved, ford" (*Old English*). A "residence" name.

Stanhope .... "From the rocky hollow" (*Old English*). A "residence" name.

Stanislaus .... "Glory of the camp" (*Slavonic*). St. Stanislaus is the patron saint of Poland.

Stanley .... Either "dweller at the stony lea" (*Old English*), or shortened from Stanislaus, above.

Stanton .... "From the stone dwelling, or quarry" (*Old English*). A "residence" name.

Stanway .... "Dweller by the stone, or paved, highway" (*Old English*). This highway might have been an old Roman road.

Stanwood .... "From the stony wood" (*Old English*). A "residence" name.

Stedman, Steadman .... "Dweller at the 'stead' or farmstead." An Anglo-Saxon "residence" name.

Stefan .... A Russian form of Stephen, below.

Stephen, Steven .... "A crown or garland" (*Greek*). St. Stephen was the first Christian martyr. DIM. Steve.

Sterling, Stirling .... "Of honest value." An Old English nickname from the sterling coins. These may have taken their name from a small star or a starling bird stamped on them.

Stewart, Stuart .... "A steward." An Anglo-Saxon "occupation" name. The steward was originally the keeper of another's estate, and particularly of the domestic animals.

Stillman .... "Quiet or gentle." An Anglo-Saxon name from the same root as our word "still."

Stilwell .... "From the still, or quiet, spring" (*Anglo-Saxon*). A "residence" name.

Stoddard .... "Stud-herder, or keeper of horses." An Old English "occupation" name.

Sumner .... "A summoner" (*Old French-Latin*). One who called, or summoned, persons to court. An "occupation" name.

Sutton .... "From the south village" (*Old English*). A "residence" name.

Swain .... "A youth"—particularly a youthful servant (*Teutonic*).

T

Taber .... Either "a taborer"—a player on a small drum (*Spanish-Arabic*); or "herald" from "tabard," a garment worn by heralds (*Old French*).

Tait .... "Cheerful" (*Scandinavian*).

Talbot .... A name probably derived from some heraldic device showing the "talbot" or bloodhound (*Old French*).

Taylor .... "A tailor" (*Old French-Latin*). An "occupation" name.

Teague .... "A poet or bard" (*Celtic*). Sometimes used as a nickname for "Irishman" because of the Irish partiality for the name.

Tearle .... "The stern." An Old English nickname.

Tedman, Tedmund .... A short form of Theodmund, meaning "protector of the nation" (*Teutonic*); or of St. Edmond, meaning "prosperous protector" (*Anglo-Saxon*).

Telford .... "Worker in iron," or literally, "iron-cutter" (*French-Latin*). An "occupation" name.

Terrence, Terence .... Either "tender" (*Latin*); or, if from the Irish, "like a tall tower." DIM. Terry.

Terrill, Tirrell .... "Martial, or Thor-like, ruler" (*Teutonic*). Thor was the Norse god of war.

Terriss, Terris .... "Son of Terry"—Terry being short for either Theodoric, or if Irish, for Terrence.

Tertius .... "The third" (*Latin*). A name given to a third child, if a son.

Thaddeus .... "The praised" (*Hebrew*). The Biblical Thaddeus was one of the twelve apostles. DIM. Tad, Thad.

Thatcher, Thacher .... "A roofer, or thatcher." An Old English "occupation" name.

Thaxter .... Same as Thatcher, above.

Thayer .... "Of the nation's army" (*Teutonic*).

Theobald .... "Bold for the people" or "patriotic" (*Teutonic*).

Theodore .... "Divine gift" (*Greek*). DIM. Ted, Teddy.

Theodoric, Theodric .... "Ruler of the people" (*Teutonic*).

Theron .... "Hunter" (*Greek*).

Thomas .... "The twin" (*Hebrew*). The Biblical Thomas was one of the twelve apostles. One legend relates that he was so named because he had a twin sister. DIM. Tom, Tommy.

Thorley .... "From Thor's lea, or meadow" (*Teutonic*). Thor was the Norse god of war.

Thornton .... "From the thorn tree farm." An Old English "residence" name.

Thorpe .... "From the small village, or hamlet" (*Teutonic*). A "residence" name.

Thurlow .... An Old English "residence" name, meaning "from Thor's hill." Thor was the Norse war-god.

Thurston .... "Thor's stone or jewel" (*Scandinavian*). Thor was the Norse god of war.

Tilden .... "From the fertile valley." An Old English "residence" name.

Tilford .... "From the good, or fertile, ford" (*Old English*). A "residence" name.

Timothy .... "Honoring God" (*Greek*). The first noted Timothy, or Timotheus, was a court musician to Alexander the Great. The Biblical Timothy was a disciple of St. Paul. DIM. Tim.

Titus .... "The safe, or saved" (*Latin*); or perhaps from a Greek word meaning "giant."

Tobias .... "Goodness of the Lord" (*Hebrew*). DIM. Toby.

Tobin .... A form of Tobias, above.

Toland .... "From the taxed land" (*Anglo-Saxon*). A "residence" name.

Tolman .... "Collector of taxes, or tolls." An Old English "occupation" name.

Tom .... Short for Thomas, above.

Tony .... Short for Anthony, which means "beyond praise" (*Latin*).

Torbert .... "Glorious as Thor" (*Teutonic*). Thor, which means "thunder," was the Norse god of war.

Torrance .... An Irish form of Terrence, which means "like a tall tower."

Torrey .... "Dweller by the tower" (*Celtic*). A "residence" name.

Townsend .... "From the end of the town." An Old English "residence" name.

Tracy, Tracey .... Either "courageous" (*Anglo-Saxon*); or "the harvester" (*Greek*).

Trahern .... "Stronger than iron" (*Celtic*).

Travers, Travis .... "From the cross-road" (*Old French-Latin*). A "residence" name.

Tremayne, Tremain .... "From the town of the stone" (*Celtic*). "Stone" here probably refers to some monument or ruin.

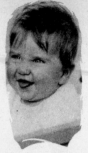

Trent .... "Dweller by the Trent." The name of the English river Trent may mean "swift running" (*Latin*).

Trevor .... "Prudent" (*Celtic*).

Tristan, Tristram .... "Sorrowful" (*Latin*). A name made famous by the knight of the King Arthur legends.

Truman .... "A faithful, or loyal, man" (*Old English*).

Tudor .... A Welsh form of Theodore, which means "divine gift" (*Greek*).

Tully .... Short for Tullus, a legendary king of Rome. The meaning of the name is lost.

Turner .... "Worker with the lathe" (*Latin*). An Old English "occupation" name. Also, if from the Old French, "champion in the tournament."

Tyler .... "Maker of tiles or bricks." An Old English "occupation" name.

Tyson .... "Son of the Teuton, or German" (*Teutonic*). The name may also be traced, through Dyson, back to Dionysos, the Greek god of wine.

U

Uland .... "From the noble land" (*Teutonic*).

Ulric, Ulrick .... Forms of Alaric, which means "ruler of all" (*Teutonic*).

Ulysses .... "The angry or wrathful" (*Greek*). The hero of Homer's "Odyssey."

Upton .... "From the high town." An Anglo-Saxon "residence" name.

Urban .... "From the city" or "urban" (*Latin*), so meaning courteous, or well-mannered, as contrasted with the rustic.

Uriah .... "The Lord is my light" (*Hebrew*).

Urian .... "From heaven" (*Greek*).

V

Vail .... "From the vale, or valley" (*French-Latin*). A "residence" name.

Val .... Short for Valentine, below.

Valdis .... "Spirited in battle" (*Teutonic*).

Valentine .... "Strong, valorous, or healthy" (*Latin*). St. Valentine is the patron saint of lovers.

Vandyke .... "Of the dike" (*Dutch*). A "residence" name.

Van Ness .... "Of the headland" (*Dutch*). A "residence" name.

Varden, Vardon .... "From the green hill" (*French-Celtic*). A "residence" name.

Varian .... "Fickle, changeable" (*Latin*).

Varick, Vareck .... Probably a form of Warrick, which see.

Varney .... "From the alder grove" (*Celtic*). A "residence" name.

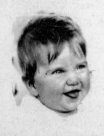

aughn .... "The small, or little." A Celtic nickname.

ernon .... Either "flourishing" (*Latin*), or a "residence" name from the town of Vernon in Normandy.

ictor .... "The conqueror" (*Latin*).

incent .... "Conquering" (*Latin*).

inson .... "Son of Vinn." "Vinn" was an Old English contraction of Vincent, above.

irgil, Vergil .... "Flourishing" (*Latin*). Made famous by Vergil, the Roman epic poet.

ivien .... "Animated" (*Latin*).

ladimir .... "World-ruler" (*Slavonic*).

olney .... "Of the people" (*Teutonic*).

W

ade .... An Anglo-Saxon personal name, meaning "one who moves"—so possibly "wanderer."

adsworth .... "From Wade's estate" (*Old English*). See Wade, above.

albridge .... "From the walled bridge" (*Old English*). A "residence" name.

alcot, Walcott .... "Dweller in the walled cottage." An Old English "residence" name.

aldemar .... "Mighty and famous" (*Teutonic*).

alden .... Either "mighty" (*Teutonic*); or, if an Old English "residence" name, it means "from the wooded valley."

Waldo .... "Powerful or mighty" (*Teutonic*).

Waldon .... "From the wooded hill" (*Old English*). A "residence" name.

Waldron .... Probably an English form of Waldran meaning "mighty raven" (*Teutonic*). For the ol significance of the raven, see Foreword.

Walford .... "From the Welshman's ford." An Old En glish "residence" name.

Walker .... "A thickener of cloth." An Old English "oc cupation" name. A "walker" walked on cloth t thicken or "full" it. The name may also mea "forester" or "walker of the king's forest."

Wallace, Wallis .... "A Welshman" (*Teutonic*). Welsh man, in turn, means "foreigner."

Walt .... Short for Walter, below; but occasionally use as a separate name.

Walter .... "Mighty warrior" (*Teutonic*). A name pop ular in various forms throughout Europe. DIM Wat, Walt.

Walton .... "From the walled, or enclosed, farmstead (*Old English*). A "residence" name.

Ward .... "Watchman, or guardian" (*Teutonic*).

Ware .... "Prudent, astute, wary" (*Anglo-Saxon*).

Warfield .... "From the field by the weir, or dam" (*Ol English*). A "residence" name.

Warford .... "From the ford by the weir, or dam." A Old English "residence" name.

Waring .... Probably meaning "true" (*Latin*); but pos sibly "heedful" (*Teutonic*).

Warner .... "Guarding warrior" (*Teutonic*).

Warren .... "Game warden" (*Teutonic*). An "occupa tion" name, which can be traced back to mea merely "protector."

Warrick, Warwick .... A famous English name, but o uncertain meaning. Possibly either "protectin ruler" (*Teutonic*), or "stronghold" (*Old English*)

Warton .... Either "from the farm by the weir" or "fro the poplar tree farm." An Old English "residence name.

202

ashington .... An Old English "residence" name. George Washington's family came from an English village originally called Wassyngton. This signifies an estate belonging to some ancient Teutonic ancestor who was nicknamed "the acute or smart."

atson .... "Son of Wat," Wat being a short form of Walter.

ayland .... "From the land by the highway" (*Old English*). A "residence" name.

ayne .... A short form of Wainwright, or "wagonmaker." An Old English "trade" name.

ebster .... "Weaver." An Old English "occupation" name.

elby .... "From the farm by the spring" (*Scandinavian*).

eldon .... "From the spring by the hill" (*Teutonic*). A "residence" name.

elford .... "From the spring by the ford." An Old English "residence" name.

ellington .... "From the prosperous estate." An Anglo-Saxon "residence" name.

ells .... "Dweller by the springs" (*Old English*). A "residence" name.

endell, Wendel .... "Wanderer"—or one who wends his way (*Teutonic*).

esley, Westley .... "From the west meadow" (*Old English*). A "residence" name. Made famous by Charles Wesley, founder of Methodism.

eston .... "From the west farmstead or village." An Old English "residence" name.

Weylin .... A contracted and varied form of O'Phela▸ which means "son of the wolf" (*Celtic*).

Whitby .... "From the white dwellings, or settlement▸ (*Scandinavian*). A "residence" name.

Whitelaw .... "From the white hill" (*Old English*). ▸ "residence" name.

Whitford .... "From the white, or clear, ford." An Ol▸ English "residence" name.

Whitney .... "From the white island." An Anglo-Saxo▸ "residence" name.

Wilbur .... "Beloved stronghold" (*Anglo-Saxon*).

Wildon .... "From the wooded hill" (*Old English*). ▸ "residence" name.

Wilford .... "From the willow tree ford" (*Old English*)▸ A "residence" name.

Wilfrid, Wilfred .... "Resolute for peace" (*Teutonic*)▸

Will .... Short for William, below.

Willard .... "Resolutely brave" (*Teutonic*).

William .... A most ancient name, the first syllable o▸ which may be traced back to one of the thre▸ primeval gods of Norse mythology. The Teutoni▸ form, Wilhelm, means "willful helm, or helmet,▸ and may be interpreted as "resolute protector." I▸ is a common, and often royal, name in all Euro▸ pean countries; and was especially popularized i▸ England by William the Conqueror. DIM. Will▸ Bill, Billy.

Willis .... "Son of Will." See William.

Wilmer, Wilmar .... "Beloved and famous" (*Teutonic*)▸

mot .... "Beloved heart" (*Teutonic*).

son .... "The son of Will." See William.

lton .... "From the farmstead by the spring" (*Old English*).

nchell .... Possibly "drawer of water." From the Anglo-Saxon "wince" (winch)—a device for hoisting water from a well.

ndsor, Winsor .... An English town name of Teutonic origin, probably meaning "at the bend of the river." During World War I the English royal family changed their original German surname, Guelf, to Windsor, from their residence, Windsor Castle.

nfield .... An Old English name which certainly means some sort of field; but whether the field was a battle-field, a pleasure-field, or a winding-field is uncertain.

nfred, Winfrid .... "Friend of peace" (*Teutonic*). St. Winfrid, whose name was later changed to St. Boniface by Pope Gregory II, was Germany's original patron saint.

nslow .... "From Wine's hill" (*Old English*). "Wine" was an Anglo-Saxon nickname signifying "the friend" or "friendly."

nston, Winton .... "From Wine's farm" (*Old English*). Compare Winslow, above.

nthrop .... "From the friendly village." A "residence" name of Teutonic derivation.

Wirt .... "Worthy" (*Anglo-Saxon*).

Wolcott, Woolcott .... Probably "dweller in Wo cottage" (*Old English*). See Wolfe, below.

Wolfe, Wolf .... "A wolf" (*Teutonic*). The wolf was adversary highly respected for cunning and cou age by primitive peoples.

Wolfram .... "Wolf-raven" (*Teutonic*). An "anim bird" name, implying one to be dreaded or spected. See Foreword.

Woodley .... "From the wooded meadow." An Old E glish "residence" name.

Woodman .... "Forester, woodcutter, or hunter." A Old English "occupation" name.

Woodrow .... "From the hedgerow by the forest." A Old English "residence" name.

Woodward .... "Forester, or keeper of the forest" (O *English*). An "occupation" name.

Worden .... Originally "Warden," "a warder or guar ian" (*Old English*).

Worthington .... "From the river-side" (*Anglo-Saxon* A "residence" name.

Wright .... "Workman"; especially a worker in wood, a carpenter. An Anglo-Saxon "occupation" nam

Wyatt, Wiatt .... "Guide." Old French forms of Guy, adopted into English.

Wylie .... Either "beguiling" (*Anglo-Saxon*), or a sho variant of William.

Wyman .... "Warrior" (*Anglo-Saxon*).

Wyndham .... "From the windy village" (*Old English* A "residence" name.

X

Xavier .... "Brilliant" (*Arabic*). The name usually co memorates St. Francis Xavier.

Xenophon .... A famous Greek historian and soldi The name may signify "strange voice."

Xerxes .... "King" (*Greek-Persian*). Xerxes was world-famous Persian conqueror.